W9-CPP-250

HURON COUNTY LIBRARY

3 6492 00487316 9

Blyth   DATE

A Man &
His Words

Robert J. Boyer

Through Changing Times

by J. Patrick Boyer

971.31604092 Boyer -B

Boyer, J.
A man & his words.

PRICE: $19.95 (3559/by   )

This small book is dedicated
in large love to . . .

PMB, RJB

MVB & AJB

. . . for the sense of belonging to
something larger than oneself.

APR 27 2004

Chapters

Copyright © 2003 Canadian Shield Communications Corporation

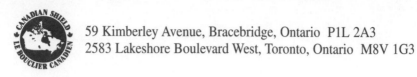

59 Kimberley Avenue, Bracebridge, Ontario P1L 2A3
2583 Lakeshore Boulevard West, Toronto, Ontario M8V 1G3

Published in Partnership with The Dundurn Group, Toronto.

All rights reserved. No part of this publication may be reproduced, stored in a retrieval system, or transmitted in any form or by any means, electronic, mechanical, photocopying, flight of bird, recording, or otherwise (except for brief passages for purposes of review) without the prior permission of Canadian Shield Communications Corporation. Permission to photocopy should be requested from the Canadian Copyright Licensing Agency 'Access'.

Designers: Chris Brevetti, Ken Adlington, Pui-Wah Jackie Cheung

National Library of Canada Cataloguing-in-Publication Data
Boyer, J. Patrick
    A Man & His Words
Includes photographs
ISBN 1-55002-486-8
Biography

Printed and bound in Canada by Pristine Printing, Toronto.
Printed on recycled paper. ♺

Foreword

The Consummate Canadian

It is an honour to write this Foreword to a book about a good friend and a great Canadian whom I have known in the many roles he has filled with distinction: patriarch, churchman, musician, politician, editor, historian, friend.

In each of these contrasting roles, he has defied all the stereotypes about what the hard-driving, tough-talking, devil-may-care dynamo is supposed to be. Yet he has achieved eminence and success in all of them. Perhaps that is why he seems the consummate Canadian.

It is not by accident that this book should be written by a son who himself is an established author, and published for the opening of a reading room presented by a daughter as a companion space to the children's library that bears his wife's name. The Boyers know they belong to each other and are proud their father and grandfather belongs to them.

Throughout his busy life, he has always "loved the Church and given himself to it," presiding at the organ and singing in the choir of his parish church through many years, his deep, rich baritone precisely modulated according to the music set. No one has really heard 'O Canada' at its best unless that person has stood beside him while he renders the national anthem as it should be sung but too seldom is.

Through his long years in the Ontario Legislature, he became a dean of the House but was respected for reasons other than that priceless luxury – electoral longevity. In all parties he was honoured for an expert knowledge of the rules, a reverence for parliamentary procedure, a love of democratic tradition, a commitment to the common good.

As longtime editor and publisher of the Bracebridge *Herald-Gazette,* he showed how a local newspaper can be an instrument for binding a community together. His literary interest going beyond the day-to-day minutiae of local events, he brought it all together in local histories that told the story of a people and the place they call home, books that should give him the title, 'Mr. Muskoka'.

It has been both a pleasure and a privilege to know Robert Boyer in all those roles and to be impressed by his record in each one. But most of all I am glad to have known him in the role so prized by so many – friend. His circle is wide because over the years he has practised the wisdom in Franklin D. Roosevelt's counsel: "If you want a friend, be a friend."

In these latter years that friendship has been enjoyed mostly in his room at The Pines, an impressive retirement community in whose establishment he played a leading role so many years ago. There he has made his home during years when he has been frail in body yet strong in mind, following Queen's Park debates by television, reading the newspapers and following current events avidly, discussing affairs with a critical mind that remains as sharp as it has been ever gentle.

What a man. What a story. What good fortune that it can be told in this fine book by someone uniquely able to tell it. Patrick Boyer has followed his father down familiar roads in retracing his life. He too has been a journalist, an author, a parliamentarian, a family man, a churchman. This book is thus the product of that rare coming together of subject and writer, a worthy tribute to a father worthy of it by the one most able to give it. Written by a master of words, it shows us a man who not only lived by words but used words to enhance the life of his community and its people.

Yet it is more. It is not only about a man and his written message. What it shows us about the man and his words shows us also the kind of Canada Robert Boyer represents. We are the country we are because of Canadians such as he.

Reginald Stackhouse
Former M.P. and Canadian Representative
to the United Nations General Assembly;
Commissioner, Ontario Human Rights Commission

1

Introduction

A Man and His Words

In the beginning was the Word. For a man of deep religious faith like Robert J. Boyer, this scriptural assertion also doubles as the coda for his life.

So much of Bob Boyer's activity and so many of his public contributions centre upon them – words read as a life-long avid reader, words written as a journalist, words type-set as a printer, words pruned and revised as an editor, words marshaled as an author, words studied in many forms and places as a researcher, words deftly deployed as a story teller, words addressed to fellow legislators and wide-spread audiences as a public speaker, words assembled in games of Scrabble and teased out of memory by difficult crossword puzzles. While some may die by the sword, Robert Boyer has always lived by the word.

His birth in 1913 began a third generation of Bracebridge writers and newspaper editors, following his grandfather James Boyer of *The Northern Advocate* and father George Boyer of *The Muskoka Herald.* Bob Boyer would live a long life at the intricate intersections of reading and writing.

Robert and Wilson Boyer would sail into a shared sea of newspaper work and musical expression, two brothers navigating separate courses from different outlooks in the same boat.

His marriage in 1940 to Patricia Mary Johnson, a clever and attractive university-educated woman who was librarian in Bracebridge and a teacher of languages, brought together as one two people who shared enthusiasm for the works of Shakespeare, music, novels dark or humorous, and the reciting from memory of long passages of poetry.

Robert and Patricia raised three children, each of whom is a writer, each of whom has employed words in music, theatre, journalism, authorship or publishing.

Over his adult years, he has edited more than four thousand editions of newspapers, written a dozen books and booklets, edited some 27 books, started three newspapers, amalgamated two others opened a bookstore.

In 2003, creation of The Robert J. Boyer Reading Room at the Bracebridge Public Library poetically united dual themes of his life – the central importance of the written word, and the imperative to serve one's community. Both are combined in the Robert J. Boyer Reading Room, a place of welcoming dignity that encourages members of the public to relax and freely enjoy the unique companionship of reading. Why this is so fitting can be appreciated the more one discovers the story behind the man and his words.

Realism required that a picture of Robert and Wilson should show what it meant to be a young Boyer in Bracebridge – dressed in tie and jacket, and poring over an open book.

2

In the Beginning

Robert James Boyer is a son of Muskoka. Born December 14, 1913, in the same Bracebridge home on north Manitoba Street where his father began life in 1879, he is a third-generation Muskokan through all four of his grandparents.

His birthplace had been built by Bob's great-grandparents, James and Hannah Boyer, around 1870. They had migrated from England to New York, then from New York to Muskoka in 1869 to claim free homestead land in Macaulay Township when Muskoka District was opening for settlement. The move to Canada meant James, having already served in the Grenadier Guards in England, was able to escape forcible conscription into the Union Army, a development causing the American Civil War riots in New York City. It was a new life in Bracebridge. With his legal training from England and New York, he drafted local bylaws as Town Clerk and served for three decades as Justice of the Peace. With his skilled calligraphy, he crafted artful

The house where Robert Boyer was born in 1913 at the north end of Bracebridge. This Boyer Family scene from the 1890s shows Bob's Grandfather James Boyer seated reading a book, beside his wife Hannah who is knitting. The young man standing at the left is their son George (who would become Bob's father). The two women in white blouses are their daughters Annie and Nellie. Another son is Fred, seated with 'Spot' Boyer. Son Charlie is absent.

testimonial addresses. With his flare for writing and organization, he became editor of the town's first newspaper, *The Northern Advocate.*

George White Boyer, one of James and Hannah's children, would marry into another of Muskoka's pioneer families, the Archers of Browning Island, Lake Muskoka. The Archers had arrived in Bracebridge the year before Confederation, in 1866. George's bride, Ethel Victoria Archer, had gone west with one of her sisters to work in a department store in Winnipeg, then returned to Bracebridge. Vic married George in 1911.

With the outbreak in 1914 of yet another war between the various imperial powers of Europe, Canadians as a part of Britain's empire were brought into the fighting. The lives of thousands of young men from Canadian schools and offices, farms and factories, fishing boats and forestry operations would for four years be expended in machine gun fire, mustard gas attacks, barbed wire snares and heavy shelling along sodden mud and corpse strewn miles of French and Belgian fields that bristling English commanders deemed worthy of another assault though no one any longer remembered why.

George enlisted at Camp Borden and immediately received his commission as a lieutenant in the Pay Corps. His second son, Wilson, was born to Victoria on May 21, 1917, just at the time George went overseas as a Captain in the Canadian Army with the 122 Muskoka Battalion. George's legs were badly burned in action in France during the war. Upon returning to Canada in August 1919 George saw his son George Wilson Boyer, now more than two years old, for the very first time. His first son, Bob, had developed a great deal during his absence, too, and was now six. George carried on with the newspaper work he'd begun in 1903, and was now at the helm of *The Muskoka Herald,* a Bracebridge weekly which succeeded *The Northern Advocate.*

The family setting of Bob Boyer's early life was steeped in fulsome religious worship and church music, community affairs and Tory politics. Whereas in politics James Boyer had been a 'Clear Grit' or 'Reformer', his son George moved to the Conservative side. Sons are not always replicas of their fathers. The political affiliation of their wives was of less importance until 1917 when women in Ontario were given the right to vote. Then Vic displayed the same vigorous enthusiasm for Conservative candidates as she did for Bracebridge hockey teams. In such a setting their son Bob turned into a Conservative, too.

A tie and jacket was his common garb, attendance at public events a routine. Reading books was as frequent as eating meals. The affairs of the newspaper became as intrinsic to Bob as breathing, since the subject was always in the air. The close connection between politics and the press, which would mark Bob's own adult career, especially when he served in the legislature and edited the local newspaper at the same time, was first displayed to him at the age of 12 years. That was when, in 1925, his father George was simultaneously editor of the Bracebridge weekly *The Muskoka Herald* and elected to be mayor of the Town.

3

Education in the School of Life

After Bob's early education in the nearby Gospel Hall primary school on the east side of north Manitoba Street, then Bracebridge Public and High schools, the Great Depression of the 1930s set in. Like so many others, the Boyers had barely enough money to scrape by.

Bracebridge was in severe economic decline after the United States raised protective tariffs to killer levels to save American jobs. Canadians lost theirs. Leather exports to the U.S. stopped. The huge tannery at Bracebridge closed. Some 600 people left town, a quarter of the population.

With businesses failing and everyone cutting their spending, advertising declined, subscriptions were cancelled, and fewer printing orders came through the door. It was increasingly hard for the Boyer newspaper business to survive. To economize, no material was wasted. Small 8-page weekly newspapers could purchase pre-printed sheets of newsprint with four generic pages of general news and national advertising on one side, and then print the other side with four pages of local news, local ads, and, of course, its own masthead and that week's date. When cut and folded, the eight pages gave readers a satisfactory blend of both the big picture and Bracebridge doings. An eight-pager was the smallest a paper could be in terms of production requirements. For hard-pressed publishers, this expedient of 'Readyprint' was a life-saving solution. Canada's smaller communities, especially as the Depression throttled the economy down, could simply not generate more than four pages of advertising and local news. It was either Readyprint, which no publisher, especially a Boyer, liked, or receivership.

Yet as subscriptions to *The Muskoka Herald* shrank, each week unused Readyprint paper from the supplier in Toronto accumulated. Trying to make ends meet, the Boyers reluctantly decided to use up this stock when printing a subsequent week's paper, hoping those few who received a paper with half the content repeated would either not notice or not care. Some readers understood that hard times forced difficult choices. Some complained and were handed one of the fully fresh editions, if a copy still remained at the newspaper office. Yet some, predictably, used the repeated serving of words as an excuse to bail. One who did was the unimpressed principal of the Bracebridge High School, George S. Johnson.

The Johnson family, newly arrived in town in 1923, marked a fresh start – a new principal for the new redbrick High School soon to be built. Johnson and his wife

Lillie Senior had met at university, and graduated together in 1905 with degrees from McMaster. His courtship included inscribing gift books of poetry for musically talented, highly literate Lillie. When they married his teaching career took them to schools in Meaford, then Whitby, then Moose Jaw, then to the Northern Academy boarding school at Montieth for students from remote northern Ontario homes and, after 1918, returning World War I vets whom the Government in Ottawa wanted to keep away from the cities. Their three daughters, Genevieve, Patricia and Stephanie, moved up through the curriculum with the older students, so they were well ahead of most learners their age when arriving in Bracebridge.

The Johnsons first took up residence in 1923 in the Lount house on McMurray Street, but moved in the spring of 1925 a few houses further north on the same street into the sprawling 'Westlawn' house built for Dr. Bridgeland around 1880, one of the first brick houses in town, with its large lawns and extensive gardens. The Lount house was demolished, making way for the new High School which workmen, starting in the spring and working six days a week from 7 a.m. to 6 p.m., completed by November the same year when Principal Johnson moved into his commanding new office. George and Lillie with their three daughters began life in town at the high end of society. The same year the new school was ready, George Boyer was elected Mayor.

Four years later the Depression began. Principal Johnson on a school salary did not face the same financial straits as those running small businesses or earning wages, although he did have upkeep of the huge Westlawn residence, not to mention three daughters and the money they'd be needing for university.

So he sent his beautiful daughter Patricia down to the newspaper office, where she met the publisher's son Robert. It was a bittersweet moment. She was some two years older, and they were barely acquainted. The attractive young woman's message to him was to cancel the Johnson subscription to his newspaper. Her father "didn't want to pay twice for the same news."

Certainly no funds would be available for Bob to go to university. Even the $10 his mother Vic earned each autumn from the Ontario Department of Agriculture to judge baking entries at the Bracebridge Fall Fair had disappeared. The newly elected Liberal Government under Premier Mitch Hepburn, after closing the Lieutenant-Governor's official residence at Chorley Park and flamboyantly auctioning off all the cabinet minister's limousines in front of Queen's Park, then scoured the province to ensure that not one single Conservative was left in any paying position – right down to the smallest amounts paid once a year to those helping with town and country fair exhibits.

A Re-scripting of Roles

Yet wily Ontarians, collectively adept at survival in an age of patronage politics, understood the advantage of a federal or two-tier system of government, and right from

Confederation on began hedging their bets by electing different political parties to Queen's Park and Ottawa. The Tories may have been out of office in Ontario, but found themselves in power under Prime Minister R. B. Bennett nationally. Cash-strapped George Boyer, prominent as a publisher and former mayor of the community, and a Tory, gratefully accepted appointment from the national Conservative Government as Customs Officer at Bracebridge.

His son Bob dutifully accepted his fate. He would work to help his family survive, and struggle for the sake of the community to keep its Tory newspaper alive, an alternative voice to *The Bracebridge Gazette* published by G.H.O. Thomas of Liberal persuasion. Robert Boyer left high school after finishing Grade 12, replacing his father George at the newspaper, as George himself moved into the Customs Office in the Post Office building.

This development had several consequences. One was that this episode fixed for all time Bob's political loyalties. He had witnessed first hand how each of his parents had been punished or rewarded, respectively, because of their party affiliation. Similar scenes re-enacted in countless households across a country with traditional party politics and its mixed blessing of patronage accounted for the intrinsically self-perpetuating nature of partisanship and, in the case of the Boyer family struggling with the Depression in 1930s Bracebridge, left its indelible Boyer impression on young Robert. When it came to the Boyer slice of bread in the hungry Depression, he saw which side it got buttered on. Party loyalty became a touchstone for the rest of Bob's life, sometimes kept quiet beneath the surface, yet seldom absent. Quite simply, he felt reassured in the company of fellow Conservatives. Like partisans everywhere he seemed prepared to overlook a number of flaws in individuals if they at least voted the right way, even though the same faults, when displayed by those who cast their lot on the Liberal side or worse, seemed magnified in his eyes. Born a Tory, and finding no reason to change, he remained loyal.

A second and far grater consequence of the roles within the Boyer family being reassigned was that the young man who so loved newspapers and the publication of words would now get full frontal exposure.

Newspaper Editor at Age 19

As the young editor launched his career in April 1933, he also expanded his involvement in the life of Bracebridge, joining in many activities, taking leadership roles in some, enthusiastically observing everything else. During 1934 and 1935, while working full time, he also took classes at the High School on McMurray Street, conveniently just two blocks away from *The Herald* newspaper office at 27 Dominion Street, successfully completing 'Senior Matriculation', or Grade 13.

In later years, Bob's first-born daughter Victoria would describe his 1930s education in these words: "Dad graduated from high school straight into the job of editing *The Muskoka Herald,* freeing up his father for a government job with a pay cheque. So Bob Boyer's post-secondary study was Bracebridge, his texts the decades of family newspaper files, his practicums participation in community organizations, his publications presented weekly for peer review."

Although denied a chance of going to university, a world whose promise he had glimpsed when earlier attending Varsity football games in Toronto and seeing with anticipation the intellectual ideal of student life on campus, Bob Boyer knew that not finding himself inside an institution of higher learning did not have to mean the end of his education. Not many young Canadians of this era made it to college, even in the best of times. The Depression ensured that would not change. In important respects, however, a serious student outside institutional structures had advantages.

Universities provided an educational focus for a fortunate few – people like the Johnson sisters Patricia and Genevieve, or 'Patsy' and 'Paddy' as they were called, who went off to McMaster University, Patsy with a scholarship at age 16 for standing top among Ontario students. Yet universities and colleges were not the only institutions of 'higher learning'. Bracebridge very early had acquired a library, begun by the Mechanics' Institute, then continued and expanded as a Carnegie Library. The Public Library was a triumph of liberal education, bringing books on all subjects to the free use of people where they lived. If some, such as Patricia Johnson, went to a big city for further education and a degree, Bob would continue his education right at home in Bracebridge, without the certificate of a degree granting institution, and minus the panache of confidence university-trained people acquire.

Already a studious reader, Bob took to books in even more purposeful fashion. His quest was made convenient by the Bracebridge Public Library now being just a short block away, and it wasn't the Library which had moved. The family financial crisis of the Depression meant the original Boyer home on north Manitoba Street had had to be sold.

A family that arrived in the 1860s for free land no longer owned any. Bob moved with his parents and brother Wils to the corner of Quebec and Dominion streets across from the newspaper office. Their new home was the rambling red brick Armstrong residence, with its wide verandah, white pillars and railings, and mauve lilac bushes beyond the front lawn at the street corner forming part of the grandeur that was Dominion Street in those days, a space befitting George who had a position of prominence in town. Yet it was rented accommodation. The threadbare Boyers maintained their personal dignity, and enjoyed their new residence in the very centre of town, but keeping up appearances was getting increasingly difficult.

The Advantages of Self-Education

For Bob in such circumstances, self-education became the only ticket. Like other men who never got all the formal education they'd once hoped for, but who knew they would go through life encountering others who had, including many with a heightened sense of self-importance, Bob made a resolute effort to see he would be just as knowledgeable even without the degree. Few who found themselves outside the structured institutions of education, however, could have hoped for better learning conditions. In addition to the neighbourhood convenience of the Bracebridge Public Library, Bob had other advantages.

Newspapers from towns all over the country poured into his office. Just as the Parliament Buildings at this time housed a Reading Room where elected representatives could scan hundreds of neatly arranged newspapers from all across Canada, Bob had, at 27 Dominion Street in Bracebridge, its local equivalent. This was the result of a custom among most weekly newspaper editors to exchange free subscriptions in order to keep up on one another, to follow trends on issues and styles in reporting, and even to emulate format improvements noted in these sister publications. In the cramped offices of *The Muskoka Herald,* these newspapers – not to mention news releases from a wide variety of organizations, other current journals and various feature pieces proffered for publication -- piled up day after day. Bob had an unrivaled source of information, and obtained daily education in the course of just doing his work. About the only thing Robert J. Boyer might have longed for, given the mishmash of papers with so many other items on the countertops and desks of the newspaper office, was a proper reading room.

Other advantages also came with this self-education territory. Unlike the experience of directed learning in university courses, a man educating himself found he was free to pick up, or put down, a book on whatever topic tweaked his interest. He could design and develop his own courses. Absent the schedule of classes, Bob could spend as much or as little time a day as he chose or had available, whether to pursue the subject or author of his current greatest interest, or to read a book that passed by happenstance into his hands and so open his mind along new channels. Bob Boyer's equanimity ("Nothing is ever as good, or as bad, as it first appears," he would say) allowed him to see the benefit of learning about things his own way. Increasingly, his quiet curiosity was treated to his own brand of scholarly discipline.

A Retentive Mind and the Power of Words

Although shy by nature, the necessity of reporting weekly on the community's life drew the youthful editor into circles and events he would not otherwise have experienced. Such a development in these still-formative years contributed to his knowledge of the community that soon reached deeper than that of most townspeople, putting him on par with police constables, telephone switchboard operators, the town clerk and the Catholic priest. Such seasoning helped Bob form an increasingly balanced and worldly-wise view of people and their doings.

The focused quality of Bob's memory also soon became apparent. Public speakers addressing local meetings would marvel how few notes the young man at the Press Table took while they addressed a Muskoka audience, yet how fulsome and accurate an account Bob Boyer had recreated for publication in the paper's next issue. He would return to his paper-cluttered Editor's office on Dominion Street and, working late into the nights, the machinery in the print shop silent, keep himself company with the clatter of keys banging out the story on an Underwood typewriter he'd taught himself to use, the smoke from his cigarette trailing upwards from the ashtray nearly buried in papers on his roll top desk.

His smoking career started in conjunction with his move from student to journalist. His father smoked, and sons will follow their dads. This was also the time when Bob joined a whole generation of readers to whom the titles of W. Somerset Maugham, the popular British novelist, playwright and short-story writer, were familiar. Maugham wrote with the sophistication of a world traveler, looking unflinchingly on humanity. His characters, if sometimes contemptuous, demonstrate an unsentimental fidelity to the full range of human motives.

A feeling Maugham once described in himself seems to have likewise been the experience of Robert Boyer in his strong attraction to reading: "I am never so happy as when a new thought occurs to me and when a new horizon gradually discovers itself in front of my eyes. When a fresh idea dawns upon me, I feel lifted up, apart from the world of men in a strange atmosphere of the spirit. It is a new freedom. I feel aloof from the world, and for the moment I am independent of all the surroundings."

Balancing a Style of Writing

As a very junior newspaperman Bob had compensated for his youth by adopting a writing style he felt reflected maturity and added dignity to the columns of his paper.

"His writing style was formal," notes his daughter Vicki, "but the spirit of the writing was as an insider. The practice of recording the positive events of the councils and boards, the churches and lodges, the families and businesses overrode any inclination for 'investigative journalism'. He wrote to honour and record his community, not expose it."

He crafted editorials in the manner of the leading British and English-language Canadian dailies he enjoyed reading, an *ex cathedra* voice of authority and seeming objectivity. Robert was circumspect in the news game. He avoided the passion of a pamphleteer, the style of journalists who deploy words as weapons to inflame.

Reading the gripping novels and short stories flowing from the sharply-honed pen of Somerset Maugham and the typewriter of Ernest Hemmingway, or any of the others serving up dramatic writing, seldom translated into any similar expression of human realities and frailties in Bob Boyer's own published articles. Generally he reported facts but was restrained when it came to feelings, an early style which largely endured throughout his life, even to the point of causing consternation for those who knew the touching drama of some events he told in his matter-of-fact fashion. A horrific Atlantic crossing of his ancestors would be reported in such phlegmatic tone that a particularly heart-wrenching tragedy, for example, was summed up for readers simply as, "The baby died on board."

As a result, over the years the community came to know only the stiffer and passive style that fitted and reinforced the public's more conventional image of a Conservative politician, a church organist, a prominent member of community organizations and fraternal societies, a man so formal and so mindful of his position in the community that as long as he was holding public office he would show his respect for it by wearing a tie and jacket to the beach.

He valued the understatement, perhaps even seeing it as a civilized antidote to the bombast prevalent in so much North American discourse. In telling stories he would quietly unfold his narrative, then wait with a hunter's patience to see if the listener had apprehended the subtle humour lurking within the harmless snare of his words. Likewise, to inform someone about a person's death or other tragic turn of events, he never exclaimed, never went for the shock effect some people so relish creating in others, never sought being the centre of ghoulish attention as a bearer of bad news others had not yet heard. He invariably conveyed bad news simply by explaining the sequence of events that led to the outcome. This fatherly fashion was a kindly way of reporting, a journalist using his pattern of disinterested presentation of important information in its context. A gentle man, this was his gentlemanly way of sparing a listener unnecessary emotion over a development that would be bleak enough for him or her to absorb. He had wisely learned that the way people respond to something very much depends upon how they are told about it.

His modesty also contributed to this general restraint in writing style. Robert J. Boyer believed a reader really needed to know about the exact location on the main street of a 1930s drug store, or who the owner's ancestors were, but appeared surprised if you suggested the reader might equally care about what he felt like going into the place, how it smelled in his nostrils and sounded in his ears sitting on a swivel chrome stool at the marble-top counter by the soda fountain. He was stolidly grounded in the Old School where one did not mix the personal into the larger picture, and cleaved to this division despite his attraction to the graphic storytelling of Maugham, Hemmingway, and others. He lived, it seemed, a compartmentalized life.

Personal Feelings, Public Writing

This was carried through into his journalism, almost as if he read with the right side of his brain and wrote from the left. Bob Boyer would not have succeeded any more as a journalist for *The Toronto Star* than Ernest Hemmingway had, though for just the opposite reasons. The understatement and factual accounts by which Bob Boyer would let the facts speak for themselves, or the visceral engagement with human reality by which Hemmingway let his readers feel for themselves, fell at the polar ends of the socially conscious human interest school of journalism housed in the editorial precincts of the *Star*. The engaged humanistic style of reporting had many readers in Muskoka where the *Star's* robust circulation spread north into the same District where Bob Boyer placed his weekly publication on offer.

While few expected the local weekly paper to read like a big city daily, their expectation of difference was certainly reinforced by a Muskoka newspaper under Bob Boyer's editorship that expressly did not mix the personal with the public. At various intervals over the decades other Muskoka papers, such as those under the focused and resourceful editorial direction of influential publishers such as Andrew McLean or Edward Britton, provided a contrast with their more turbulent and sometimes caustic stir-'em-up styles, which only served to demonstrate at closer range for Muskokans how the public temperature in a community can be regulated by who is giving the weather reports. Bob Boyer didn't usually bother people with severe storm warnings, because from his perspective mostly he expected only a summer shower.

Not that all of his writing resembled perfunctory council minutes engrossed by some township clerk, by any means. Bob Boyer had acquired deeply held convictions about Canada and its institutions, and about the importance of people and their practical needs. In politics, despite his adherence to forms and formalities, he also was possessed of a democrat's instinct to look to the real needs of those who live and work daily to make our country function. The religious tradition in the Boyer family, which was principally Methodist, further reinforced this instinct. The close-to-the-ground realism of this activist and open-eyed Protestant denomination embraced moral uplift in society and adhered to the social gospel in daily life: one's religious duty was to uphold any person who suffers inequalities or injustices in human society because all of us are equals before God. Each of these influences worked its way deeply into Bob Boyer's outlook, and so in turn, his actions. Among those actions, because he was a journalist and newspaper editor, was writing.

When he did allow his feelings to be provoked or moved, they could give rise to words that truly tingled and inspired. In 'the morgue', as newspaper folk call the stored sequential accumulation of past issues of a newspaper, can be found occasional editorials by Robert J. Boyer worthy of entry in any Canadian creative writing competition. Sometimes his children would show such an editorial to one another, "Wow! Look at this. Can you believe Dad wrote something as great as that?"

Bob, even if circumspect as an editor, was at least not confined the way other citizens often find themselves, feeling they "must write a letter-to-the-editor" to ventilate their annoyance or frustration or outline a better solution. That was his life-long joy of being a newspaper publisher! He had at hand a ready outlet for the expression of ideas, for the presentation of features on local developments, and from time to time for special 'Progress Editions'.

His first big progress edition was published in many sections, printed with a coloured front page to mark the 'progress' of Bracebridge with the opening of the new Bracebridge Memorial Arena in 1949. Another was a special edition produced for the town's 100th anniversary in 1975, which chronicled a century of Bracebridge institutions, elected and volunteer community leaders, churches, service clubs, sports teams, businesses, and major events. The yearly Christmas number was always a big feature for advertising, special articles, and, beginning in the late Fifties, a front page dedicated entirely, not to news, but a full-size picture of a Muskoka Christmas scene. The New Year's edition recorded highlights of the year just concluded, with photos that captured poignant moments, columns of type with dates and events parading in a month-by-month retrospective, and an editorial which looked back to evaluate and ahead to anticipate the community's state of affairs.

The editor of a community's newspaper is a craftsman in many ways, especially the art of fostering particular attitudes and using information not just to report upon but also to create the local culture. Robert Boyer did not say this. He did it.

Robert Boyer and his father George, along the Muskoka River on board Bert Brown's fuel boat Peerless II, in the late 1940s.

4

The Personal Adventure of Private Reading

The image of a newspaper editor and publisher as a flamboyant public personality lives in the imprint of literature and the imagination of movies. In practice, however, it is too easy to mistake something in print as being the same as the individual who wrote it. Bob Boyer appeared regularly before his community in the newspaper, but behind the paper and his coverage of events, remained a particularly private man.

At an early age he had joined the local chapters of closed societies for fraternal and religious life, hiving off from not only the public but even his own family those parts of himself that relished whatever it is that occurs among members of the Independent Order of Odd Fellows and the Masonic Order to provide secret passage to higher understanding, private bonding, and spiritual reward. In 1935, at age 22, he was admitted to Bracebridge Lodge, Odd Fellows, and was later appointed to Grand Lodge offices. He became a member of Muskoka Lodge, A.F. & A.M., and eventually achieved 32nd degree in Scottish Rite, for example.

In his newspaper writing, and in the books he both read and wrote, and in his public life as an elected representative, Bob Boyer drew a privacy line, almost instinctively it would seem, between the personal and the public. So did many others in the culture of those earlier times, a trait rendered all the more noticeable as they grow older and stand out in a North American society where now virtually nothing is private and the most personal dimensions of human life are celebrated and cross-examined under the media microscope for entertainment of the emotions more than improvement of the mind.

In this approach of personal circumspection in journalism Bob was influenced by his father George. Despite his worldly outlook – conveying the impression of not only forgiving people's foibles but even being amused by them, – George W. Boyer almost never allowed a person's slip or indiscretion to be reported in the newspaper. He kindly but firmly stated that to do so would hurt feelings and harm the reputation of local families.

For each issue of the newspaper Bob had to decide what warranted coverage, what stories should be spiked, and where the contentious line needed to be drawn between an individual's right to privacy and the public's right to know. This was his responsibility, as it is the work of every newspaper editor, in a practising democracy.

Robert Boyer and his companion books and newspapers were inseparable. These candid shots are just a sampling from a life-long album of the same. In an easy chair above The Herald-Gzaette *newspaper office, he reads a newspaper.*

By Roselyn Castle in September 1970, he holds his ever-present book while his daughter Vicki observes her children Johnson and Martha Billingsley preferring to ride atop the car.

All the while his deeper pleasure, and his private self, came freely to life in the words which others had decided to write and publish. For beyond the formal veneer of his newspaper writing, and behind his instinct to retain through privacy the secure inner domain of his spiritual life, dwelt another layer of Bob's personality. Bob Boyer would always have a book on the go. Almost addicted to reading, he'd always have a worthy volume just within arm's reach, ready to pick up if a spare moment presented itself. Why not? Books were mood altering and mind expanding.

Family photographs show him on vacation, whether standing at Stone Henge or sitting by a motel pool in South Carolina to walking with pigeons on Trafalgar Square or approaching the Parliament Buildings in Ottawa, always with a companion book in hand. To visit his new parents-in-law but sit alone in an August Sunday's garden reading a book of history in the company of hollyhocks beneath dappled sunlit boughs,* or to unfold a deck chair in preparation for settling in with a novel,** was to be Robert Boyer in action. Each new book held the exciting prospect of becoming his passport to a fresh adventure. It had been this way from the start.

The Book Stays in the Library!

From his earliest years of reading, Bob vicariously lived these adventures through novels that transported him down back alleys, through dread and death, espionage and high drama, racy encounters and earthy language. The enduring appeal of a good murder story captured Bob for the first time when he was about ten years old. Among the stories he heard about where those written by Jack London, the novelist who had grown up in dire poverty, had become an adventurer in the Klondike, a hobo and a sailor all by age 20, and in his own self-education had been influenced by the works of Darwin, Marx and Nietzsche.

When Bob appeared at the Bracebridge Public Library to borrow *The Call of the Wild,* one of London's books, the censorial librarian, Hattie Dickie, prohibited him from seeing such a work. Here we see the vital influence of librarians, which almost always remains understated because it is so far reaching. We may not recognize the full impact such guardians of the world's canon of literature have upon us, effortlessly guiding and molding us: a eyebrow raised at a proffered selection brought to the check-out counter; a joyful nod when pushing a volume across the reading table where one is studying and communicating without words a secret about the timely importance of this key work she has thoughtfully selected; a stern look across the top of reading glasses as her radar vision picks up a youth snickering at dictionary definitions of adult practices; or even the hushed words "You may want to browse along this aisle" as if tipping one off to where the real treasures were hidden.

Such influence of a Bracebridge Public Librarian reinforced the notable division between Bob Boyer's public prose and private reading. At a time when the Bolshevik

---

* *See front cover of book.* ** *Back cover.*

Revolution in Russia and the Winnipeg General Strike had recently taken place, she forbade the church-going young man access to a work by a socialist whose books were marked by sympathy with the poor and prophecies for world revolution with an emphasis on the primitive, the powerful, and the cruel, and a predilection for the violent. Raw life was clearly something boys in Bracebridge should not encounter before full maturity reached outside literature. Or perhaps she had not so deeply immersed herself in the social and political consequences of the transaction taking place in front of her, but simply judged the book by her own morality and its cover the same way she judged its putative borrower by his age. Although a puritan might have been alarmed by such a siren title as *Call of the Wild,* it was the story of a dog. The dog's name was Buck.

Robert Boyer in 1925 was 12-years old, reflective and formal. By this date, his father was Mayor of Bracebridge, and his reading tastes clashed with the librarian's approval rating.

Yet the boys of Bracebridge, well known to be as adept as those elsewhere in circumnavigating the shoals of fusty morality, commonly chatting among themselves about how they understand public libraries to be the foundation of a free and democratic society even if a librarian with her hair in too tight a bun didn't, also knew that the Public Library was not the only show in town. In Bob's particular case, his equal devotion to newspaper reading provided an excellent alternative avenue by which to detour his education around the narrowness of the controlling adult at the checkout desk.

The Star Weekly at that time was running serialized novels, and with the sensationalism that has always been a hallmark of *Toronto Star* journalism, seemed less concerned about protecting its readers from dark reality than selling them more copies of its publication. Even before Librarian Dickie had glared sharply across the top of her eyeglasses, visually scolding the deviant ten-year old for his salacious reading tastes, Bob Boyer had in fact already read Agatha Christie's very first novel, *The Murder of Roger Ackroyd,* in weekly installments.

When doing so, he had come across a passage in her novel describing the problems of an unmarried woman who was having a baby. The puzzled boy asked his Grandfather Archer, "Can a woman who is not married have a baby?" The older man looked at his grandson a moment, then replied, "Oh, I'll tell you. When a baby's going to come, it's going to come!" For the rest of his life, Bob would consider that wise and timeless generalization "a pretty good answer."

From that day in 1923 at Bracebridge Public Library when his freedom to read a Jack London novel had been denied by a person in authority who implicitly shamed him for his taste in books, Bob kept the pleasures of his reading – whether novels or – histories, biographies or poetry – behind brown paper wrappers, as it were. No greater fan existed of paperback books than he. Casually available in stores used to selling unwashed members of the general public their personal requirement items, the paperback rack was Everyman's satellite library. For little money and no hassle Bob could pick out Mickey Spillane's latest grizzly thriller and walk home to enjoy a good read without having to justify his tastes to anyone else's moral code.

Perhaps as a personal balancing act, Bob in his private time, which he claimed for himself daily despite all the jobs he simultaneously fulfilled during his life, gave full reign to his true love for reading. Here he could freely select, and the choices were always rich and diverse.

When money became available, he joined a Book Club that monthly brought him the latest best sellers. Over the years Bob has slipped daily into the whodunit universes created by Agatha Christie, Sir Arthur Conan Doyle, Angela Thirkell, Studs Terkel, Mickey Spillane, Ellis Peters, Martha Grimes, Dorothy I. Sayers, Alistair Maclean, William Deverell, John Ralston Saul, Frederick Forsyth, Jack Higgins, Ken Follett, John Gardner, Reginald Hill, Len Deighton, Robert Ludlum, John Le Caré, Andrew M. Greeley, and dozens more and their many hundreds of books. These masters of realism and nemesis, of irony and surprise, unfolded the darker layers of human drama and brought Bob into direct contact with the force of powerful writing.

Bob's reading interests extended far beyond crime fiction. He almost seemed, to those who observed such practices at close quarters, to oscillate according to a private formula, his own version of a lifetime reading plan: two detective stories then one serious work of history or biography. Reference works were close at hand, and a new word or unknown allusion was immediately tracked down, never delayed to be checked later. Pursuit of new meanings was a game, the sport of a self-educating man. Matters ranging from church liturgy to the sequence of monarchial succession in late 1600s England would be pursued avidly, "read and inwardly digested."

At Stone Henge in England, Robert enjoys the moment by anticipating reading the book he carries.

When Bob moved his residence to Bracebridge Villa west of town in the 1990s, the dominant feature of his small room was this reading chair with good bright light. In this same photo, an Anton Pieck picture of 'The Printing Shop' can be seen behind Bob on the wall – a gift from his daughter-in-law Corinne whose own father Gerard had been a printer and Linotype operator in The Netherlands.

The Shakespeare canon was so familiar to him that Bob could quote long passages from memory, and the complete works of social critics who conveyed their message to a wider audience under the cloak of dramatic humour, such as Charles Dickens and Stephen Leacock, were just as well known.

Historical novels became a pleasing genre, combining as they did several of Bob's interests in a single work. So books flowing from such prolific authors as R.F. Delderfield, Robert Goddart, John Gallsworthy and Howard Spring, who set their dramas in a richly textured immediacy of times past, would engage him in educational entertainment.

Other interests of Bob's, such as historical, biographical, military and political affairs, intersected in the many compelling and authoritative works by that Englishman who primarily wrote for a living, brilliantly and authoritatively, but who also engaged fully in British public and political affairs, Winston S. Churchill.

Books have always been Bob Boyer's companions, his non-electronic internet. In the early days when he was learning about the world, books pulled him forward through his extensive self-education. In the sprawling decades of his adult life, books provided a brief sanctuary from the endless needs and demands of people whom it is the duty of someone in public life and elected office to address. In the long years after his wife Patricia died and many of his friends and contemporaries received the last rites of a newspaperman – obituaries penned by Bob for his increasing number of friends and acquaintances who one by one crossed through the mists to the other side of the River – books were still there. Old friends and new best sellers alike, books did not die. At worst they just go out of print, or get lost.

Yet even so, the memory of them remained. To hold up before him, without saying a word, a book he had not seen for years was to witness in Bob Boyer's face the warming sunrise expression of joy that is born at the unexpected reunion of old acquaintances. The rush of fond memories immediately flooded over all else. Then a storehouse of his recollections would fuel a remarkable conversation, connected immediately to the genesis, impact and importance of this old friend.

One such experience came with the booklet *At Christmas Be Merry,* which he had compiled in 1946 from writings by Washington Irving (the author from whose book the town of Bracebridge got its name) about 'Christmas at Bracebridge Hall', along with other seasonal poems and woodcuts, printed to also show townspeople in the postwar years the high quality of typesetting and lithography available locally. He hadn't seen that small publication for decades, but it came to light when his son was "clearing to the walls" the Kimberley Avenue home Bob and Patsy purchased in 1956 and where papers and booklets had lain undisturbed for decades in cupboards. The special nature of this publication and people's warm reaction to it sparked a re-print in 1998. What was both nostalgic and attractive in 1946 became even more so half a century on.

In an age when an individual's privacy rights have been so eroded by inquisitive governments and invasive computer users, the last best bastion of freedom is reading. It fulfills the ultimate privacy right, for in the domain of reading each individual is sovereign, a crown made from treasures of the mind, held in place by the personal choices and private moments of connection with our priceless inheritance of world literature in its enriching diversity.

Visiting Browning Island in Lake Muskoka was a great occasion to sit with son Patrick's wife, Corinne, who loved reading newspapers as voraciously as he did.

5

Public Speaking and the Printed Word

B ob's father George Boyer spoke in public with ease. He advised a would-be orator to meet one's audience in order to gauge right on the spot its changing moods in relation to other speakers and the larger events of the day, so as to then be able to create a speech of just the right tone and nature for those assembled. Yet sons are not always replicas of their fathers.

Both Bob's shyness and his increasing skills in writing for publication meant he would appear at meetings he was expected to address with a prepared text. He would then invariably read it at his audience, regardless of its size or mood. This practice also served to buttress him against criticism of the kind he'd once received early in his career for an address that was rather off the cuff, from a crusty individual who'd "expected more".

The MPP for Muskoka speaks at the Huntsville Legion Hall on November 27, 1959, as Hon. George Wardrope, Ontario's Minister of Highways, applauds behind the flowers. The microphone is from Huntsville's new radio station CKAR.

Public speaking became a regular part of Bob Boyer's life. Here he addresses friends and fellow Rotarians at a club meeting in Holiday House, Bracebridge, reporting on some of the major reforms being implemented in Ontario by the Robarts Government.

More positively, Bob was influenced by the practice of Winston Churchill, who rallied the British peoples and the free world against the Axis powers in the early 1940s in part by the force of his speeches. Every word of those galvanizing addresses, he knew from his reading of Churchill's books, Churchill had carefully written and revised and rehearsed in advance.

After the War, and as he himself began to take a larger leadership role in public affairs locally, Bob Boyer believed that when he had a proposition to advance or a major proposal to unveil, it was "best to write it out clearly and read it at the meeting." This became his own self-reinforcing practice, whether at church meetings, Rotary, in the Ontario Legislature, or at Muskoka District municipal meetings.

The result was that Bob Boyer's speeches were substantive, well researched, authoritative. Of course that contributed further to his image and public reputation as a somewhat stiff if stalwart man who found it awkward to relax and have fun in public. Yet it did mean, too, that he always delivered the message he thought appropriate to the occasion. Invariably that message included a more substantial dose of local history than audiences may have been expecting to get, or certainly than they could receive from other quarters, a sharing of the past more appealing to older rather than younger members of most audiences.

Yet that was certainly not the end of it. Virtually all his speeches had two audiences. The public speaker, after all, was also the editor and author. At the conclusion of each such address to a particular audience, Bob Boyer had in hand for a much wider readership a text suitable for a feature article in a future edition of his newspaper and, in time, the basis for a chapter in one of his many books. His father George, perhaps a more affable and engaging public orator, only managed to get one book written – *Early Days in Muskoka,* in 1970 – and even at that it was based on a series of radio addresses he had painstakingly prepared for broadcast over Huntsville's CKAR radio station. By then the man who had proffered advice about public speaking to his son had learned a different lesson about the writing of books from him.

In this steady fashion, year after year, Bob succeeded in recording a vast story of Muskoka and its people, events of local history, and the public policies and programs of government by which aspiration became reality. As his years advanced, it became commonplace for him to hear himself referred to as the greatest living authority on Muskoka, and by friend Reg Stackhouse, himself a man of letters, as 'Mr. Muskoka'. This was the legacy of his decades of engaged experience, but also a gift of his unfailing memory. As Bob's daughter Alison, who edited his book *Bracebridge Around 1930* for publication, wrote in her editor's note to that work, "R.J.B.'s richly detailed description of earlier times presented in this book is text for the most part written from his impeccable memory."

What he tells newspaper reporters, researching authors, individuals digging up their family roots, old friends and rising generations of students, is the same information he has dutifully and clearly recorded in his many books. Several of these have now in fact become classic reference works for those seeking information about the District he documented from the ground up.

The Books of Robert J. Boyer

Books by Robert J. Boyer were mostly written at times of other major responsibilities in his life. Experience as an editor of a weekly newspaper, steadily producing news stories, editorial comments and feature articles for print while also carrying out other duties, helped him do what seemed impossible to many others.

At Christmas Be Merry (1946, reprinted 1998)
One Hundred Years: A Centennial History of Bracebridge United Church (1961)
A Good Town Grew Here, (1975, expanded edition 2002)
Celebrating a Ninetieth Birthday (1977)
Early Exploration and Surveying of Muskoka District (1979)
History of Ryde Township (1979)
Pictorial History of Woodchester Villa (1982)
Bracebridge Horticultural Society History (1982)
History of St. Thomas' Anglican Church (1983)
Fifty Years Above Self in Our Town: 50th Anniversary History of Bracebridge Rotary Club (1986)
Power from Water (1994)
Bracebridge Around 1930: Youthful Memories of Muskoka's District Town (2001)

Some of these publications coincided with anniversaries, always a good focus for a writer and a fine peg for a book. *A Good Town Grew Here,* despite its generic title that might also have been claimed for a book of local history by a thousand other municipalities across North America, appeared in conjunction with the Bracebridge municipal centennial in 1975. *Power from Water* was published in 1994 to mark the centenary of Bracebridge municipal electric generation and water works, Robert Boyer proudly chronicling the story of how the Good Town came to be the very first to own and operate its own electric power system in 1894, after local ratepayers had approved, in a referendum conducted by Town Clerk James Boyer, takeover by the municipal government of a privately owned power station at the foot of the Bracebridge Falls. In this same fashion, on the occasion of his mother Victoria's 90th birthday, Robert wrote an extensive history, with many family portraits included – a handsome booklet on her life and ancestral heritage, including the personalities and progresses of the Archer and Boyer families.

"Steady but sure" is how he did it. Until limitation of his mobility in his eighties, Bob Boyer was noted for the regularity of his church attendance, most often as a choir member. Regular church attendance became a pattern in the rhythms of his life. Also from the structured existence of his Army experience to his religious observance of the scheduled routines of the Legislature, from the studied practices of his fraternal affiliations and regular weekly and monthly meetings for many other organizations of which he was a participating member, not to mention the short-cycle demands of publishing a weekly newspaper over much of his lifetime, Bob found comfort in the ordered life.

In fact, the practice of order was essential for accomplishment. His routines and personal discipline in adhering to them directly accounted for his ability to do so much. How many can go upstairs to bed, part-way through the televised drama of a Saturday night movie, just because it's 11 o'clock and that is their regular hour to retire? Perhaps someone who knows the ending because he's already read the book?

As his second-born daughter Alison observed, "My father and I are born in the Chinese astrological year of the Ox. Dad and I typify these strong, steady creatures with our work ethic of 'slow but sure'. My father especially has proved his great propensity for monumental tasks with his valuable and in-depth documentation of Bracebridge and Muskoka history."

In writing these historical accounts, Robert Boyer did not gloss over hardship or reality. His own accounts present some unvarnished stories of local calamities and personal tragedies. While he did not sensationalize events, neither did he duck reality. When a sequel to his book *A Good Town Grew Here* was being written by a whole team of authors to cover the decades from World War I to present times, he was displeased with the attempt to pretend that only good times rolled. The municipality and its people had passed through a bitter and blighting decade and a-half of devastating economic depression and world war. To not be accurate about that did a disservice to the many people, of whom he had been one, who hung in for better days. Telling that truth rather than blithely avoiding it was the honest way to truly boost the reputation of the community, in his considered view. Although himself an ardent supporter of the Town and its good works, Bob disdained what might be called a Chamber-of-Commerce outlook or boosterism mentality that sought to present Bracebridge history only through rose coloured glasses. Like his late wife Patricia, he is an optimistic realist.

Robert J. Boyer has crafted a legacy encapsulated in a body of writing that will only increase in value as the decades mount. His writing in most recent years has begun to reflect a little more the twinkle in his eye and the shy smile of the quiet storyteller who lets the humour of an event sink in softly. His daughter Vicki, writing about her father in the book Alison crafted, noted of his writing style that his family was "delighted to notice more boyish mischief creeping into his earlier stories", versions that "give us the feeling of a young fellow showing us the shortcuts and alleyways around well-known haunts." If the "dignified editor of the Thirties had to grow up early," she said, "the elder statesman can now chuckle", adding how one can now "treasure the chance to grin with him."

In ways as deliberate as they were unassuming, Bob Boyer made a monumental contribution through his words and works that ultimately did not require him to be boastful or self-asserting because in their cumulative effect they spoke with a forceful eloquence that is rare – the message implicit in the accomplished deed.

Increasingly at ease in public speaking, but invariably with some prepared text in hand, Bob Boyer and Hon. Charles S. MacNaughton, Ontario's Minister of Highways, officiate in the opening of new highway and bridge construction at Bala.

6

The Art Forms of a Printer

W hile Bob Boyer was becoming publicly prominent as a weekly newspaperman, the editor and publisher from 1933 of *The Muskoka Herald,* behind the scenes there was also the skilled technical requirement of actually producing the newspaper itself. The paper occupied about half the time in the print shop, the rest for job printing which helped cross-subsidize the newspaper costs.

At age 19, Bob had also become manager of the commercial printing department at *The Herald* office, although even from age 17 he was able to set type and, if careful, slowly run a job printing press. Now that school was over for Bob and Wils, Vic helped, not with their schoolwork but their workload at the newspaper office. Bob's mother took charge in the 1930s of the financial records, making up the invoices for advertisements in the paper, and looking after the classified ads. She became very connected with the merchants and others working in the community, as a result of these contacts, and became a founding member of the Bracebridge Business & Professional Women.

Here another side of him came to the fore, the artist. Bob truly relished the life of a printer: setting type, composing headings, preparing illustrations, making up the pages, operating the printing presses, the newspaper folding and book binding equipment . . . in short, the graphic arts.

Over his own lifetime, the graphic arts would go through three revolutionary transformations. At the start of Bob's printing career, the images reproduced on paper came from ink on type. Type was a physical thing one worked with. It came as large wooden letters placed together for dramatic newspaper headlines or urgent public notice posters. It was also the metal letters selected by hand from cases of different 'fonts' or sizes and styles and reused time and time again in the fashion known to all printers dating from the German Johann Gutenberg's first invention of moveable type and printing in 1440, a year arbitrarily chosen as the date of the accomplishment, credited to him but on which he and others in several European countries were all experimenting at the time. Printer Gutenberg organized all the elements of printing as a process – type production, ink manufacture, the press, paper supply – into a coherent whole. The printing of books took off, with demand from students at the growing number of European universities and development of new reliable forms of paper.

Once the printing press had been mechanized printers turned to the matter of supply of type, type composition, and distribution of individual types after use. There had to be better ways than hand composition, and the inventive human mind triumphed again when complete mechanization of type casting came with William Church's casting machine in 1822. It could form 3,000 individual pieces of type per hour. Print shops everywhere acquired more and more type, stored in dozens of wooden pull-out cases with open-top compartments, each the exclusive storage space of the waiting pre-formed individual letters, numerals and spaces (all the *e's* in one place, all the *s's* and *m's* and so on in others) in front of which men sat or stood by the hour setting type in small hand-held adjustable metal trays called 'sticks'. Bob Boyer, like his brother Wils, father George, grandfather James and son James Patrick, became proficient in hand composition of type. For, this method was still used into mid-20th Century for many of the specialized fonts of display type.

Rapid mass typesetting, however, had become a totally different matter, thanks to the invention by Ottmar Mergenthaler of the Linotype machine in 1884. This remarkable invention set lines of type from liquid metal (a melted alloy of lead, tin and antimony). The indicate and complex Linotype machine vastly sped up the process, giving rise to bigger newspapers and more books, and bequeathing the term 'hot metal' type to differentiate, for printers, the new method of setting type by machine from the earlier ways of setting the type from individual pieces of metal, a separate one for each letter or space, by hand.

In addition to the Linotype, other hot-metal typesetting machines such as the Intertype (a direct competitor) and the Monotype and Ludlow each used the same basic principle of individual matrices or moulds cast from a harder metal like brass (the same principle as in casting coins or medals) arranged into lines of characters that spelled out the text to be typeset, then a casting made with the lead alloy. Printers' lead was soft enough to work with but hard enough to take thousands of poundings in the printing press as inked impressions of it were repeatedly imprinted upon paper.

Over the years the Boyer printing plant and newspaper office acquired a number of Linotypes, an Intertype, and a Ludlow. These costly typesetting machines were purchased at great financial risk by The Muskoka Publishing Company for its operations at 27 Dominion Street. Each of them Bob operated skillfully, and respectfully, after losing the tip of a middle finger to a Linotype in 1934.

Bob would happily lose himself in their operation as he created the text and design for advertisements, book pages, or newspaper features with the same exquisite satisfaction a chef might experience pulling a glorious cake from his oven or a tailor stitching the most elegant and daring gown at his sewing machine. Like other typesetters, he could work endlessly in satisfaction at these machines, or under great pressure of a publishing deadline when all skills blended in extreme performance – the pilot who enjoys flying high in calm skies, but who can bring the craft in safely through a buffeting storm. It would be wrong to equate someone of a bookish nature with unmanliness, and Bob Boyer was proof of that. Like a chef, tailor or pilot he was an artisan and technician combined.

He was adept in the operation of printing machinery, loved the physical work of it, and thrived on its creative dimensions that provided direct expression of his own considerable aptitudes. In adulthood his non-sporting life was not for lack of interest, but of time and opportunity. Since age 17 he had been working in the print shop while still a student, from 19 was fully responsible for both it and the newspaper, and thereafter the ever-increasing press of duties would always be answered because his conscience would yank him back to work from even the briefest respite for leisure. No baseball for Bob. Yet hard work and devotion to duty was its our pleasurable reward. He was especially happy by 1937 that more typesetting and printing were required because he had the newspaper operation on a better financial footing where 'Readyprint', to his relief, became a thing of the past.

A typesetter and printer is an artisan who knows more technical skills and tricks of the trade than could ever be printed in a book. A printer understands and applies the physical attributes and interactions of metals, wood, inks, papers, humidity, temperature and pressure. A printer knows the mechanical and technical operation of dozens of machines and pieces of equipment. A printer understands the 'message' or content of what is being printed and therefore the most compelling and artistic way to compose, lay out, and print it.

A printer is above all a magician, able to bring forth a smudge free sheet of printed paper, or a clean and crisply bound book, from a printing plant with oiled machines, greasy moving parts, smears of ink and the general grime of any industrial plant. It may not be the most immaculate conception, but it is a mysteriously clean birth.

Printers can only pull off such magical transformations of words on paper because they work to the musical sound of the tinkling linotypes and the deep base rhythms of the printing presses, accentuated by the syncopated sounds of paper folding machines and the bony whine of circular saw blades cutting through heavy metal stereotype castings with more exhilarating resonance than any electric guitar ever brought crazed fans to their feet.

Printers excel because they work in an exciting place that encourages its own unique cult of excellence, a bonding of sounds and smells and heat from the machinery; the raw prospect that any one of a thousand things could go wrong in a flash as super-sensitive equipment jams or a fleck of dirt or torn sheet of paper brings a complex process to a shuddering standstill; and, above all, from the heady fragrance of from ink and paper and hot metal and oil stained wooden floors that blend into a printer's elixir more heady and intoxicating than the thickest swirl of incense around the highest alter could ever be.

No wonder Bob Boyer, companion in fraternal societies, so cherished the universal bond shared by those inducted on the basis of merit alone into the Universal Order of the Print Shop. Few vocations could so completely integrate the main forces of a man's life, the intellectual and physical, the sensual and artistic, the economic and communicative, the creative and practical. One could go to heaven, or better still, one could be a Printer.

All this changed with the advent of 'cold type'. Just as Bob and others in his family had learned each of the several ways of preparing a 'form' or page of type for printing in a 'letterpress', and had to change with new printing techniques, the early introduction of computers brought a revolution to the graphic arts once again.

The costly Linotype machines were displaced by keyboards at which girls with grade 10 educations replaced skilled typesetters. They now only had to make tapes punched with holes that corresponded to letters, and when these were run through another machine, out came columns of print that could simply be 'pasted up' on a cardboard page for printing the newspaper.

Since this also meant there was no letter to press, when inked, against the paper, gone too were the letterpresses and all the skills and technical apparatus that went with that arm of printing. This 'cold type' process was itself part and parcel of the new development in printing presses, the 'offset' method. A complete changeover to this method of production occurred at the Boyer printing plant, with Bob very much a part of this transition, learning and applying new skills.

All this changed, yet again, with the advent of 'electronic type' and the advances of computer technology. Now entire newspapers could be assembled on computer screens. Because capital equipment required to start up a newspaper was no longer the barrier it had once been, many more small newspapers appeared on the scene. The economics of weekly newspapers, or 'community' papers as they had been rechristened, changed also.

Ottawa decided to cut the subsidized postal rates that had supported the mailing of local papers. That had been how the Government of Canada did its bit to provide 'peace, order and good government' in the country, ensuring that the cornerstone of a democratic society, its independent local newspapers, would be encouraged to circulate, create identity, and air issues. Such policies, and the values they expressed, got ploughed under in the new quest for 'efficiency' in government.

After much higher costs imposed by the Post Office for mailing community newspapers came the second blow of this double-whammy from Ottawa. The Post Office, having grown complacent about its monopoly over the delivery of mail and parcels. inattentively forfeited the lucrative end of its business to courier companies which moved in and scooped its operations. Advent of facsimile and e-mail technologies further accelerated the demise of the traditional postal operation.

Rather than declaring 'mission complete', however, the battered remnants of the Post Office decided to make money delivering junk mail. For low rates the posties would carry colourfully printed flyers to the doors of every household along their postal walk. This was good for the printing business, but not for the weekly newspapers. The latter found their advertising accounts gutted as national grocery chains, electronics companies, automotive stores and so many others spent their millions of advertising dollars outside the pages of the community newspapers which increasingly struggled to serve their communities.

Some weeklies responded by striking a deal with these national advertisers. They would package these flyers along with a general interest free newspaper that, wrapped together in plastic, could be flung in the general direction of homes and office buildings up and down the streets of town. More than a breach of municipal bylaws against littering, this was an end-game salute to what weekly newspapers of Canada had been in their noble heyday.

Bob Boyer saw all this occur. In the move to free newspapers he was at the vanguard with creation of *The Muskoka Sun.* In the packaging of toss away papers, such as *The Advance* and *The Week-Ender,* he reluctantly thought the development made economic sense, although by the time this stage in the evolution of weekly newspapers came along, that decision was in the hands of others who now had ownership of the local papers.

Gone as well now were the sounds and smells that uniquely identified a place as a print shop. Something of the soul of newspapers came to be lost, it seemed, when they could be produced in spaces of fluorescent lights and strange silence, save for the hollow clatter of 'inputting' on plastic keyboards, that resembled business offices more than typesetting plants of old. Journalists no longer rushed in to bang out a story tight against the looming deadline, or even shouted details of a disaster into a pay phone near the scene so the reporter on desk duty could type the horror as the story came in. Instead, reporters simply tap 'send' from wherever they find themselves with a laptop computer, their full text transported effortlessly and instantly through cyberspace, ready for on-line editing or formatting electronically right into the page.

Once again, the man changed with his times. Bob learned many of these new skills, acquiring familiarity with the new equipment. Whichever the method, however, and by whatever techniques modernization brought in its wake, the one constant for Bob always was his pride in turning out newspaper pages with solid and informative content and artistic presentation.

His long hours of devotion to *The Muskoka Sun* tabloid newspaper, both sitting at his typewriter popularizing more accounts of early Muskoka days and standing on the concrete floor at the angled counter doing the 'make-up' of its dozens of pages (some issues exceeding 100 pages, he'd note with pride) may have been tiring. Even so, they were also exhilarating. At any stage in the evolution of the graphic arts, at any age in his seven decades in the print shop, Bob Boyer found joy in perfecting the art forms of a printer. His ability to do this reflected both his profound grasp of the essentials of the graphic arts, ranging from an appreciation for appropriate combinations of typefaces to the exquisite eloquence of white space, and on to the powers of human engagement through quality typography.

It is not enough to write good accounts and chose the right words to suit one's meaning; it is equality important, as Bob understood and practised, to give words an appearance that attracts the human eye. He enjoyed the skill of typography and printing, and regarded it as an art form.

The editor leans on the counter where he would artfully make-up pages for newspapers such as The Muskoka Sun. *Earlier in his printing career Bob Boyer worked with other techniques for setting type and making up pages with metal.*

7

The Editor
and the Librarian

Through his far-ranging community newspaper work, Robert Boyer made friendships that would long continue, even as his career evolved into electoral politics. The network of newspaper correspondents from the rural centres provided both happy personal contacts and valuable local knowledge alike, which strengthened his later public service as an elected representative for Muskoka District in Ontario's legislative assembly. Even better, he married the correspondent for the Bracebridge Public Library – librarian Patricia M. Johnson.

This union was by no means a sure thing, despite how closely love would entwine their lives eventually. After canceling her family's subscription to his paper, and leaving town for three years to attend university in Hamilton, then being absent a further period to teach school in Bancroft, Patricia had returned, more captivating than ever. The 16-year old Patsy who had won a university scholarship, and become prominent in debating and drama on campus, also discovered the fun in life, at the expense of her traditionally high marks. By the time she and her sister Paddy graduated from McMaster in 1932, they had reached the age at which most young women today enter college. Among their learning at McMaster they had come to relish intelligent fun.

Patricia Mary Johnson graduates from McMaster University, age 19.

During her absence, Bob remained a shy bachelor. With the pressures of work he had little social life, apart from the quiet pleasures of reading, a notable exception being a Bracebridge dance he attended with Conservative leader Earl Rowe's daughter Jean – tall, dark, attractive and captivatingly reserved in nature yet at ease with fun-loving laughter.

Now that Patricia was again in town, he found himself in unwanted, though understandable, competition for her attention. They might never have gotten together had it not been for the newspaper. The two shared a weekly encounter at the newspaper office, when Patricia came by to submit Bracebridge Public Library columns to the same young editor she had delivered a less pleasing message to several years earlier. Robert was happy to see that, with her daughter's columns now appearing in *The Muskoka Herald,* Mrs. Johnson had taken out a new subscription.

Editing and producing Patricia's writing was a definite connection between them. He was impressed with how well she wrote. This shared experience, encouraged by her enticing smile, suggested there should perhaps be more. Robert eagerly showed up at the Johnson residence, at the invitation of Patricia's mother Lillie, to listen to phonograph records of classical music, only to discover other bachelor suitors already seated in the front parlour with the women of the family for an evening of appreciating Patricia under the guise of serious musical study. It was clear Robert and Patricia had a mutual love of music. Yet this gave him no particular edge, for others eligible bachelors present, such as the agile and talented Leslie Tennant, were just as devoted to music. Yet where there's a will, a writer will find a means to express it.

Patricia Johnson, high heels on an old stump in summer, shortly before marrying.

Taking a drive together on Muskoka's winding and hilly country roads proved a more suitable venue for melting ice than the Baptist austerity of 'Westlawn', the Johnson home administered by its matriarch. A particular road near Bangor Lodge, cutting across the fields and up a breathtakingly steep hill, was such a challenge to the driver that at the top, despite having only moonlight to see by, Patricia insisted Bob pull the car to the side of the road so that she could properly reward his heroic driving. Their wedding took place on Saturday, November 23, 1940, the Bracebridge Baptist Church decorated with the autumn's last boughs of crimson and gold Maple leaves.

Any doubts Patricia had about how closely she might become entwined with Bob's newspaper work vanished when the couple converted the second floor meeting hall of *The Herald* building into their apartment. The redbrick structure had been erected in 1891, and the 'Herald Hall' was the upstairs part for

On a late November Saturday of 1940, in a world divided by war, Patricia and Robert become united in marriage.

meetings where three fraternal lodges held regular meetings in the pre-World War I years, then a business college occupied the space for a couple years, and in 1930 the Pentecostal Church began its local services. Just the place for newlyweds!

Several walls were put in to make it resemble living quarters, although the rough pine floorboards would still inject slivers into bare feet. Right below, the typesetting machines clacked and the printing presses rumbled. The stairs led right down every morning to work. On the other hand, a romantic couple did not have to wait until the end of day, since it might be necessary to go upstairs to get a cup of coffee or retreat there to quietly read some galley proofs at various intervals throughout the day.

As an Arts graduate from M c M a s t e r University, Patricia

As the 'Gay Nineties' return to Bracebridge, Patsy and Bob Boyer step out for good times strolling on the streets of town.

also had a flare for writing and a love for theatre and literature, a further passion that united the couple.

From the time she and Bob married, Patricia's personal life and career became inseparable. "She didn't worry about her role as a woman," reflected her daughter Vicki looking back years later. "She just got on with being supportive, in the most positive and fulfilling sense, in a productive partnership."

With the onset of World War II in 1939, Robert remained on the home front as a newspaper editor for the early years of conflict. He could be typically pictured* enjoying a quiet respite for reading at 'Westlawn', home of his bride Patricia, on a Sunday afternoon, a 28-year-old man uncomfortably mindful he was not in uniform. Yet the Government at Ottawa considered those publishing the country's newspapers, whether big city dailies or small town weeklies, to be an integral part of the war effort in keeping Canadians in patriotic frame of mind for the long siege. Editors moving

into the Armed Forces were seen as being unnecessarily disruptive of the national communications network, which at the time consisted of newspapers, only one national broadcasting network (CBC Radio), and local radio stations in larger cities. In our present era of three national television networks, dozens of TV channels through cable or satellite, two national and many regional radio networks, and the Internet, it is harder for some to fully appreciate the influential role which newspapers performed in the days when Bob Boyer was an editor from 1933 on into the war years.

As still bleaker days of war descended, Bob too enlisted. Joining the Canadian Army, he found himself launched into an experience that provided a memorable few years of his life. Serving in Canada with the Royal Canadian Ordnance Corps, he soon found the away-from-home equivalent to attending university that many young men were getting in these grim yet purposeful days.

Robert Boyer served during World War II with the Canadian Army's Ordnance Corps, stationed at Longue Pointe Ordnance Depot near Montreal.

* See front cover photo, August 16, 1941 - while World War rages and his wife is days from delivering their first baby.

The man of words found, in addition to Ordnance Corps work supplying the Canadian Forces with materiél for combat, that his prior newspaper experience did not have to be left behind in Bracebridge. In the Army Bob Boyer became editor of *The Longue Pointer,* the news and features publication of the regiments stationed at the Canadian Forces base in Longue Pointe, Quebec. Not only that, his skills as a Linotype operator could be converted into a supplemental pay cheque at one of the printing plants in Montreal during his time off the base.

His life from Bracebridge was even being replicated in Canada's premier city on the musical front. Robert joined a choir which sang along with the large Elgar Choir in the uplifting and ornate majesty of Notre Dame Cathedral in the heart of old Montreal.

During Robert's wartime absence from Bracebridge, Patricia became editor of *The Muskoka Herald,* his brother Wilson managed the printing plant, and his mother Victoria took full charge of the business office.

Patricia did not skip a beat as she slid into the editor's empty chair. "My earliest memories," recounted Vicki, "are of toddling from her desk to the old Linotype with her copy to be set as she churned out news reports and her early column 'The Roundtowner' with child under foot." A signature of initials, in the newspaper style of the period, is how columnists, hinting a blended coyness of superiority and thin mask of anonymity, appeared to readers. At this time in the early 1940s Patricia's identity as 'PMB' began with the byline she retained throughout her journalistic career.

At least the Boyers were not forced to endure the anxious wartime separation of other couples divided by an ocean, or worse. Bob was only as far away as Montreal, unlike his new brother-in-law Jim MacNaughtan who in uniform had married Patsy's youngest sister Stevie then gone overseas to front-line fighting in Sicily and next Holland. His work at the Longue Pointe Ordnance Depot entailed shipping the tanks, munitions, jeeps, arms, military supplies of every kind on their grim convoy runs to Canadian troops in the theatres of combat overseas.

His occasional furloughs permitted a train ride home to Bracebridge, where he'd be greeted down at the station by Patsy and their young daughter. Vicki squeezed her mother's hand for courage as the immense locomotive pulled into the platform, all loud black metal and noise with steam pouring from its nostrils and scaring her, a fright she braved in order to see her Daddy step down on the platform in front of them in his soldier's uniform.

Robert returned happily to Bracebridge on furlough by train during the war. At Longue Pointe he is with a fellow soldier and friend.

So it went, and the war progressed. When every last available cartridge had been shipped to Europe for D-Day, Bob again got home leave. He and Patsy were, as it joyously turned out, able to celebrate news of the June 1944 Normandy landings together. At last, battle had been joined on the western front against Hitler's iron forces. It was a sensational experience!

Nine months later, on March 4, 1945, their second child arrived, named James after his great-grandfather and Patrick after his mother Patricia. In an era when only men were thought capable of running newspapers, the boy's birth sparked a headline in the Ontario Weekly Newspaper Association newsletter, one which was gleefully repeated in a number of weekly papers across the province, going roughly for the same sensational impact of a tabloid headline 'Woman Impregnated by Whale!' This headline, equally designed to tantalize readers who would think it impossible, proclaimed: 'Editor Gives Birth to Sturdy Son'.

The printed details explained that the infant was, however, the son of a wartime *woman* editor. Even more remarkable! Once the article itself disclosed that the event was not a hoax about some sexual impossibility, but the natural act of "his war-time editor Mommy", its author went on to beamingly express confidence that the newborn boy would "someday follow in his family's footsteps as the fourth generation of Boyer newspaper editors in Bracebridge."

Robert, again home on leave in early August 1945,

George W. Boyer and grand-daughter Vicki, Robert J. Boyer and son Patrick, with Patricia's sister Genevieve 'Paddy' Johnson, beside Lake Muskoka on a Sunday afternoon.

*Robert Boyer and his daughter Vicki climbed Beaumont Mountain
to get a better view of Muskoka together.*

*At Gravenhurst's Gull Lake Park in
1948, the Librarian and the Editor are
happy with their first two children,
Patricia holding her namesake son
Patrick, while Robert, still wearing his
Army shorts, still seems in awe and
admiration that his daughter Vicki can
actually stand on her own.*

had spent a few days with Patsy, Vicki, his new son, and other family members, and was returning to Montreal by train. At Toronto Union Station, he began walking along the platform to the train when a kid selling papers shouted, "New Bomb for the Japs! Read all about it!" He bought a copy of *The Toronto Telegram,* boarded the train, and in the coach awaiting his departure, in the heat of the afternoon sun streaming through the window, held open the Tuesday afternoon, August 7th Extra Edition of *The Tely.*

The words on the page imprinted themselves into his mind. The Americans had dropped an atomic bomb on Hiroshima. "We are now prepared to obliterate more rapidly and completely every productive enterprise the Japanese have above ground in any city," United States President Truman had said. "We shall destroy their docks, the factories, and their communications. If they do not now accept our terms they may expect a rain of ruin from the air, the like of which has never been seen on this earth." The world had changed forever. Bob felt an awful sense of trepidation. He also knew the war would now quickly be over.

Robert and Patricia settled down for the long-awaited peace, together with many bright prospects ahead. On August 1, 1949, their daughter Alison Joan was born, Robert impressing his first two children with his previously undisclosed ability to cook half-inch thick pancakes one foot in diameter, while awaiting the homecoming of mother and newborn. If you can print many pages on the press at once then cut them into a smaller format, can you not make one big pancake and cut it up afterwards?

While Patricia provided a stable anchor for their family of three children, she allowed them, with courageous love, to grow independently to their own destinations. "Many a mother has quaked inwardly thinking of her son's gallant wrestling with the elements on a winter camp or a canoe trip," she wrote in a 1974 column clearly drawn directly from her own experienced feelings and thoughts, "but she has also gratefully realized that her little boy was becoming a man."

For Bob's part, the increasing public demands on his time in the post-war years meant he was content with knowing that his children were becoming free-standing and self-reliant individuals.

From the necessity of wartime editing, Patsy continued to write for the newspaper after peace came in 1945. She enjoyed the opportunity for constructive comment and creativity as a regular columnist. As 'PMB' as her 'The Roundtowner' and 'My Place in the Sun' would appear over the next three decades. Informative and pleasantly challenging columns.

Patricia assumed an important role, adding to the Boyer newspapers both a breezy literary quality and a rich understanding of human psychology, expressed in universal terms and applied in the particular immediacy of the local community. She had an inventive flare for the dramatic story, a creative sense for the touching detail, a wisdom from which to extract the salient message.

Robert, like his own father, returning to Bracebridge at the end of the previous war against Germany and its allies, continued with the publishing and printing business of The Muskoka Publishing Company. The business expanded. The local competitor was purchased as a business and married as a newspaper, christened *The Herald-Gazette,* in 1955. This was the same time Bob and Patsy purchased a house on Kimberley Avenue, that Bob took a leadership role in creating Santa's Village, and that he was elected to the Ontario Legislature as Member for Muskoka.

Bob and Patsy's children, Patrick and Alison, might have been reading a book in the early Fifties but instead were studying a small turtle, seated at the front of their Boyer grandparents home on Dominion Street.

Some Men of the Family. Robert Boyer sits on the rooftop patio created when the newspaper office on Dominion Street was expanded by a larger printing plant, in conversation with his father George and son Patrick. Two different shots portray the next generation, with Bob and Patrick, Douglas and Johnson Billingsley (Vicki's husband and their son), one standing together at Bracebridge, another in concentrated 'thinking' at Cyrus Eaton's Thinkers' Lodge in Pugwash, Nova Scotia, during a family reunion there.

8

Music as Language

Robert Boyer, great at reading books, was equally adept in reading music. If words occupied his mental energies, it was music that nurtured his soul.

Like others of his family, early in life he became devoted to music, especially singing. His mother Victoria, a pianist and church organist, taught Bob piano. His father George, choirmaster in the Bracebridge United Church where both his sons sang, began Bob in choir work in 1929. In time Bob became a bass soloist, notably in performances of Handle's *Messiah*. During the War, when he was stationed at Longue Pointe with the Ordnance Corps, Bob thrilled to sing in a large choir in Montreal's majestic Notre Dame cathedral.

After the war, in 1946, Bob and Patricia joined other enthusiastic musical performers in the Bracebridge Choral Society. They shared a love of music, and with Bob's brother Wilson and Patsy's sister Paddy Johnson, choruses would be practised while the dishes from a family meal were washed, madrigals worked out at the piano, outfits and props manufactured, and elegant costumes ordered from Malabar's in Toronto and stored in Bob and Patsy's flat over the newspaper office because it was handy next door to the Town Hall theatre.

Bob's singing talents enjoyed a full outlet for expression in roles in Gilbert & Sullivan productions such as 'Trial by Jury', 'The Mikado', 'H.M.S. Pinafore', 'The Pirates of Penzance' and 'Iolanthe', in which he sang such roles as 'General Stanley', 'Koko', and 'Lord Chancellor'. The 'patter' songs, in which Bob particularly specialized in these G & S musicals, required a skillful singer who could fire out words like a machine gun, the biggest difference from rap music of today being clarity of enunciation and precision of expression.

In one G & S production, Wils Boyer brought the performance to a temporary standstill with laughter from audience and cast alike when he pulled out, in the opening pirate scene, a specially printed copy of *The Muskoka Herald* with a screaming wooden-block bold headline PIRATES ARRIVE IN TOWN!

When the carillon system was installed at Bracebridge United Church, Robert initiated a chime concert before the Sunday evening service. A family ritual, following Sunday lunch, was his selection at the home piano of the recital pieces for that evening. Tunes were chosen appropriate to the liturgical calendar, with explanations to whichever family members were about.

In time both his daughters Vicki and Alison would play the same organ, but in these early days it was his elder daughter who followed this ritual most closely. She wondered whether people throughout town hearing the Sunday evening bells chiming a particular hymn in observance of Trinity Sunday, or Candlemas, or Ascensiontide, really truly understood its significance.

When the Legislature was in session and Bob had to return to Toronto right after Sunday supper, Vicki was permitted to play the evening concerts. However, she had not yet fully absorbed her father's art in choosing the tunes. She was "pulled back to full paternal guidance," she recalls, "after independently deciding that the playing of 'God Save the Queen' was appropriate to the 24th of May." Late-rushers to church heard the national anthem. "Compelled by the music to bolt to attention in their tracks, they eventually arrived at service in mood neither patriotic nor worshipful. Father resumed his training efforts."

Bob and Patsy's two daughters continued the family tradition of musical expression, each advancing through ever-higher levels of both music theory and musical practice with the examinations of the Royal Conservatory of Music in Toronto, each performing on the public stage from the Gull Lake 'Concert in the Park' to the 'Mariposa Folk Festival' and beyond.

Alison in particular lived her life around music, as her father had built his around words, and became a composer, lyricist, and professional performing musician. In turn Alison's daughter Bronwyn grew into an accomplished musical performer, actress, artist and writer, finding her own creative ways to skillfully blend the family talents she inherited.

After he retired from the political life, Bob had more time to pursue his abiding interest in church music. He became organist and choir leader at St. Thomas' Anglican Church, a chance to display and expand his considerable knowledge of the liturgical music he both studied and played. A particular joy was work on advent services, and his late afternoon choral service at Christmastime gave a Bracebridge version of the meditative interludes he'd found in British cathedrals.

He also expressed a sedate musical humour in appropriate ways, playing a classical sounding version of 'Canadian Boat Song' for the wedding of the McGuffins who were to paddle across Canada; a Bach-like arrangement of 'Daisy, Daisy, Give Me Your Answer, Do' for the postlude at the funeral service for his longtime friend Daisy Murphy; regimental hymn tunes for the funeral of a Vet.

9

Bringing Fairy Tales to Life

T he fairy tales in children's books can, at least around Bracebridge, become the realities of adults.

Robert Boyer was one of a small group of local businessmen who decided to respond to the early 1950s construction of the Highway 11 Bracebridge bypass, on the east side of the town, by creating a major theme park tourist attraction on the opposite side of town. Their idea was that the increasingly heavy highway through-traffic clogging the main street should certainly be diverted around the town, but Bracebridge also needed to ensure it would not in the process lose the tourist traffic that had long been its lifeblood.

The creative solution took the form of establishing Santa's Village west of Bracebridge on the Muskoka River. First proposed by community-minded citizens Mr. and Mrs. Edward W. Reid and Mr. and Mrs. Douglas Smith, who had picked up the idea on a trip through the United States, the proposal was challenging. The project for a Santa's Village appealed, yet since no local organization would adopt such a project, the matter stalled.

Santa's Village was always a place Robert Boyer, its first president in 1955, enjoyed showing to visitors. This couple, with Santa and Robert, are Gerard and Margaret Mudde, from The Netherlands, parents of Patrick Boyer's wife Corinne. Gerard Mudde, like Bob Boyer, was a printer and typesetter.

Then, encouraged by Bank of Nova Scotia branch manager I. Yorke Murphy and others, Robert Boyer wrote to a number of townspeople and called a meeting at which he advocated incorporating a company to carry out the Santa's Village proposal. The meeting promptly named him president, with Roy Garwood, Doug Wells, Clarence Green and Timmy Allchin also on the board. Bob thus served as the first president in the period when Santa's Village Limited company shares were sold, buildings designed and constructed, personnel and merchandizing policies adopted, and key staff hired.

They moved fast, and within one year a newly constructed tourist attraction was ready. Canada's newest celebrity, young Marilyn Bell who had just become the first swimmer to conquer Lake Ontario, swam from Bracebridge Bay downriver to emerge amidst cheering fans at Santa's Village on a bright and sunny 24th of May, 1955. Among the thousands on hand was the towering Leslie M. Frost, Premier of Ontario, who beamed as he spoke to officially open the Bracebridge summer home, half-way between the equator and the North Pole, of Santa and Mrs. Claus.

Many of the storybook characters beloved by children of all ages came to life from their pages in the enchanted woods of Santa's Village. Alice found herself at the Mad Hatter's Tea Party. Little Miss Muffet was scared right off her tuffet by a giant spider stringing itself down beside her from a Muskoka pine tree. Robin Hood left Maid Marion behind in Sherwood Forest to instead teach attractive teenage girls the very best way to hold a bow and pull the arrow all the way back. The magical Goose Who Laid The Golden Egg turned out to be real, after all. Santa, if you pulled his whiskers, was as authentic as they come.

Getting an overview was always important for Robert, in whatever task engaged him – the intense work of each week's newspaper, the research for his detailed history book about Bracebridge, the swirl of problems raised by constituents when he was MPP, or even the route ahead on the Trans-Canada Highway when driving the family along Lake Superior's northern shore.

10

Into the Political Arena

M ajor events seem to come in a rush. That same year, indeed the very month after getting Santa's Village launched, Robert J. Boyer, as a supporter of the Progressive Conservative Party, was elected in June, 1955, as Member for Muskoka in the Legislative Assembly of Ontario.

Despite the increased public demands on his time, Bob also continued as editor of the newspaper. Moreover, in this same period, the Boyer publication was combined with the second weekly paper of the town, *The Bracebridge Gazette,* when the Boyer family purchased and amalgamated it with *The Muskoka Herald.* Up to that time, Bracebridge had resembled the small Ontario town of 'Mariposa' with its two rival newspapers, one Tory and the other Grit, as sketched in the novels of Stephen Leacock. In the year Tory Bob Boyer was elected, the Conservative newspaper in Bracebridge absorbed the Liberal publication and prosperity seemed assured.

Bob, an ardent son of Muskoka, achieved personal fulfillment in representing the District he knew and loved so proudly in the legislature of the province. These 16 years formed a period of building and restoring, following the slowdown of the Depression of the 1930s and the war years.

By 1955 the Boyer Family was ready for Bob's first campaign for elected office. Against the solid Canadian Shield rocky background near Bracebridge Falls, the Tory candidate exudes a rare happy self-confidence, holds the hand of his daughter Alison, while Patrick and Vicki perch high and ready for action, and Patricia proudly anticipates the adventure that awaits.

Within the first year of his election to Queen's Park, Bob Boyer (extreme right) joined other Members for the Ontario Legislative tour of Niagara Falls. Here they gather outside Toronto's Royal York Hotel on March 17, 1956. In those days the Legislative Assembly was only in session a number of weeks each year, and such educational tours – another was to mines and paper mills in Northern Ontario – helped the MPPs, many from small towns in scattered parts of Ontario, get to know the province for which they were legislating, and the outlooks of their elected colleagues, better.

Linked between provincial cabinet ministers with their departmental officials and Muskoka's numerous municipal councils, representative Boyer worked closely and co-operatively with them all. Their mutual efforts brought new programs and services to benefit Muskokans, from better highways to expanded hospital services. Every Muskoka municipality benefited from new school construction. The province undertook several rural road developments as well as reconstructing and widening the highways.

In addition to his part in these advances, as member of the legislature Bob was instrumental in the establishment in Muskoka of The Pines Home for the Aged, the Ontario Fire College, new buildings for the work of provincial ministries, Port Carling locks renewal and new control dams on rivers, reorganization of municipal and educational government.

In 1962 he was appointed second vice-chairman, and later first vice-chairman, of the Ontario Hydro Electric Power Commission, participating in the historic decisions during the period Hydro moved into the major new realm of generating power with nuclear reactors.

Modernization of the structures of local government was certainly one of his greatest challenges, given resistance to change. Because of his courage and vision in

Robert Boyer, Member of the Ontario Legislature, elected representative for the District of Muskoka.

battling this change through, Muskoka's 28 municipal councils — many of them small, weak, and easily divided in the face of emerging issues of a modernizing society and expanding economy — were reorganized into six with the advent of 'District Government'.

A supporter of the Progressive Conservative party and its provincial governments, Bob walked forward happily on both legs of the Canadian political philosophy embraced within his party's name - 'progress' for him having equal importance with 'conserving'. He was re-elected in the provincial general elections of 1959, 1963 and 1967, with increased majorities each time.

He retired from public life in 1971, both as the elected representative of Muskoka and as a member of the Ontario

The family was growing up together, as displayed in this photo for the 1959 Ontario general election, printed on a postcard for Bob Boyer's second campaign. Whether it was his family support, his own hard work, the progress and prosperity policies of Leslie Frost's Government, the electoral system, or some combination of all the above, Robert J. Boyer was re-elected with an increased majority that June.

Hydro Commission, not because he was weary of serving Muskoka or because he feared defeat in an election – just the contrary. He simply understood that the way of renewal comes by those in office standing down and making room for new blood, fresh ideas, and youthful energy.

Later, in his eighties, he quipped: "Over the many decades of my long life I have seen a great deal of progress – most of it strongly resisted at the time!"

Schoolgirls from Muskoka visit Queen's Park in Toronto for an educational tour, learning that their elected representative Robert Boyer even had box lunches for his constituents.

Post-war prosperity meant heavier Highway 11 traffic running along the main streets of Gravenhurst, Bracebridge and Huntsville, so Ontario's Department of Highways built by-passes around each town to alleviate congestion and speed commerce and travel. Here Bob Boyer MPP and Huntsville municipal officials ceremonially assist Highways Minister George Wardrope cut a ribbon to officially open the Huntsville By-Pass on November 27, 1959. Patricia Boyer follows the action, second from right. Though a fairly traditional man, Bob Boyer here is on the vanguard of a new style for public officials by the late Fifties – he is the only hatless person present.

A third job, in addition to being Editor of The Herald-Gazette *and Member of the Legislature for Muskoka, is taken on by Robert Boyer in 1962. Appointed a vice-chairman of the Ontario Hydro Electric Power Commission by Premier John Robarts, he is welcomed to his new wood-paneled office on the 16th Floor of the Hydro Building, at 620 University Avenue in Toronto, by Hydro's Chairman Ross Strike.*

Bob Boyer's re-election campaigns attracted many volunteer workers, and inspired some who would to later run for public office themselves. In the top left photo, Frank Miller appears happy with the returns which Bob is checking election night, while in the top right scene, son Patrick is at his father's side on election night as a call is placed from campaign headquarters.

The lower picture, on the night of September 4th, 1984, was turn-about time, as now Robert Boyer stands at his son's right hand when Patrick was winning election to the House of Commons in his first campaign. Sons follow their fathers. This was the third generation of Bracebridge Boyers elected to office: George as Mayor, Robert as Provincial Member, Patrick as Federal Member (in a Toronto riding because Stan Darling had resolved to hold onto the Muskoka-Parry Sound federal constituency a long while yet.)

Elected members stay close to their constituents by attending community events. Bob Boyer and his federal counterpart, Gordon H. Aiken M.P. evolved an effective and mutually respectful working relationship. Shown above, they ride together in the October 1967 'Cavalcade of Colour' parade.

Below, Bob and Gordon's successor in the federal Parry Sound-Muskoka constituency, Stan Darling, attend a 1970s Fall Fair in Bracebridge, dwarfed by prize pumpkins. No longer in public office at this time, Bob Boyer still enjoyed the fall fairs, another Boyer Family tradition since his grandfather James Boyer had taken agricultural displays from Muskoka to other centres from Owen Sound to Ottawa, and Bob's father George had been President of the Ontario Association of Agricultural Societies, and his mother Vic been a fall fair judge. This was how the connection with Stan Darling had first been made decades earlier, as he also served as President of the O.A.A.S.

11

Back Out of Public Life

F ew roles in life are easy, but one of the most invidious is being the spouse of an elected representative. Supporting Robert with devotion, Patricia patiently endured in lonely absence his many years in the Ontario Legislature and his preoccupation with events around Muskoka District. Meanwhile, she remained focused on working hard to achieve specific goals to benefit others. "There is no limit to the good a person can do if you do not worry about who gets the credit," she would cheerily say.

After Bob Boyer's retirement from public office she was surprised that nothing was done by the local Tory organization to recognize his significant public service, especially since they had volunteered to her that it would be. Finally, months later, a meeting did take place. Expecting this was the event, she prepared notes for an address. Nothing happened! She felt angered by the indifference of the Conservatives to the public career of a man who had given so much to his local Party through four elections and 16 years, a non-event only made worse by Bob's almost obsequious pursuit of modesty. Both her husband and her son, who would later follow his father's example and serve in elected public office as a member of the House of Commons for a decade, might have told her that no one should ever expect gratitude in politics. Yet she was, in truth, only expecting courtesy.

Driven to exasperation and frustration, Patricia responded the way writers do best: she wrote her own account of the Boyer years of service as MPP, entitled *My Bob . . . and Muskoka's*. So fearful was she that if her husband discovered the work-in-progress he would, in his very implementation of her own rule on not caring about who gets credit, have caused printing of the small booklet to be hauled off the presses. So in collaboration with Wayne Scott, typesetter and foreman at the printing office, she clandestinely got her version produced behind the publisher's back, a story written with genuine affection. She presented to him as a *fait accomplish.*

Patricia Boyer made it clear this was not a history, nor an authoritative book, nor even a comprehensive study of the 16 years of representation by Bob Boyer in the Ontario Legislature, and it clearly is not. It was instead "the tribute to a Muskoka man who loves and serves his District and for those years he served it in a special way." Her text, she said, was "set down in love by the one who knows best what it was like."

Bob's leaving of public life was accomplished quietly and, she added, "as befits his personality, modestly." She wanted to pay tribute to "the accomplishments of those years and to the spirit of devotion that helped in their achievement." Her dedication of the small booklet to their children acknowledged the inexplicable emptiness that often lurks backstage of the very engaging public scenes of political theatre: *"To Vicki, Patrick and Alison, who through their growing years, sometimes in disappointment and bewilderment, but always in love and pride, gave their father to Muskoka and to Ontario."*

There is no better way for the story to be told than in the words of "his loving wife".

My Bob . . . and Muskoka's

by Patricia M. Boyer

In February 1955, an event suddenly changed the course of our lives and so began the period of 16 years that I wish to recall now.

During the ten years since the end of the war, Bob had returned from active service with the R.C.O.C. to the newspaper business, and I had returned from my wartime editorship to the routine of domesticity. Our lives had settled happily into a modest community pattern, augmenting the weekly publication of *The Muskoka Herald* with activity in the town, in the United Church, the Oddfellows Lodge, the Rotary Club, and the newly organized Choral Society. There were highlights: the welcoming of a third child to our family; the fun and satisfaction of the Gilbert and Sullivan presentations, when Bob's singing of "Major-General Stanley," "Ko-Ko," and "The Lord Chancellor" provided a sparkling promise of a new and pleasurable musical hobby. And we began the negotiations which resulted in the establishment, in 1955, of *The Herald-Gazette*.

There was another new interest developed, very demanding and quite exciting, when Bob joined with several other community-minded citizens for the explorations which led to the establishment of Santa's Village on the Muskoka River in 1955. This took courage and imagination, and the confidence to persuade others to invest in Muskoka. As its first president Bob enjoyed the challenge of bringing something new and attractive to Bracebridge as a tourist activity.

Then Bob was asked to let his name stand for nomination for the Provincial Legislature, a seat vacant for several months since the resignation of Hon. Arthur Welsh. Redistribution had also made a change, and the riding which for some years had included part of Ontario County was now all Muskoka. With considerable awe I heard the suggestion, and with increasing excitement approached the date of the nomination meeting.

That convention on February 26th was a cliffhanger. The Town Hall in Bracebridge was packed and the voting went right down to the fourth ballot. At that, Bob's margin of victory was two votes. Slim though it was, Bob accepted the responsibility thus handed to him by the Muskoka Conservatives, and embarked on a new career.

During the weeks that followed, until the election on June 9th, the task of becoming acquainted throughout Muskoka was Bob's main effort. It had its great difficulties; there was not on hand a predecessor with experience as a member to give counsel or support. Though a third-generation Muskoka man, and, as a newspaper editor, enjoying familiarity in certain areas, in parts of the District Bob was relatively unknown. And this had to be accomplished in three and a half months. At the same time, because there was no sitting member for Muskoka, as the nominee of the party forming the provincial government, he was already required to undertake some of the responsibilities that later became his. It was a severe initiation.

But it was also a joyful one. Through those weeks, as happened through the following years, there were countless incidents of helpfulness and hospitality around Muskoka. Old friends and those newly met in the campaign generously assisted in the process of introduction; and in many a home there was a happy meal among new friends, beginning an association deeply cherished ever since.

And so it was that on June 9th Bob Boyer, with a modest but comfortable majority, was elected as Muskoka's member of the Provincial Parliament representing the district he has always studied and loved, and supporting the Conservative party which has commanded his life-long and active loyalty. He was elected to carry a heavy load of responsibility and work; but this was entirely consistent with Bob's personal habits of devotion to duty and selfless application to the task to be done.

There opened then before him, and his family, the exciting and exacting call of public life, the beginning of a 16-year career that brought its share of achievements, and its large measure of warm friendships and memorable experience.

FOR MUSKOKA

On June 10th we were driving to Huntsville to care for some of the multiple details that were involved with the aftermath of the election campaign. The countryside was at the rapturous stage of fresh green growth under a clear blue sky that we expect in June. And that day it had a new significance. For Muskoka now, both its beauty and its problems, was definitely Bob's! This was the first of many, many such rides we took together through the district, with the feeling that this district held a special challenge and evoked a special affection from the Boyers.

During the election campaign Bob had stated that his prime aim as a member would be to see that the benefits available under the Frost government should be fully available to the people of Muskoka. That was no idle promise.

Foremost among the responsibilities calling for his time and influence was the specific one of helping Muskoka people, as a part of Ontario. The legislation in 1955 was already progressing fast in the field of assistance for individuals, and advanced steadily. Civil servants, of course, have played a major role in the local successful administration of this assistance, but the influence of the member can often facilitate action. Frequently it happens that a person feels the approachability of their member more intimately than that of office staff. The red tape that is essential can often be most quickly untangled by one person. The cordial relationships between Bob and the provincial cabinet ministers were the means of real help to Muskoka people and Councils.

Most of this work is extremely confidential. The public is unaware of it except where there has been personal experience, or an individual has made it known. Nor is the member's wife aware of it until quietly made so by the frequent repetition of individuals' spoken thanks "for what Bob did for me." Matters of this kind are not undertaken in order to receive thanks; but the many times that someone made such an expression form one of the warm memories of those 16 years, and give tangible evidence, in the record of memory, that the election promise of '55 was not empty.

Not, of course, that there was one hundred percent satisfaction! It happens for the most part that a choice to be made is not between good and bad, but between good and better; or between bad and not so bad. And almost always such a choice leaves somebody unhappy. That is why the demands on a person in a responsible decision-making position can be so arduous; and why the supportive understanding of friends and associates is so important. It is also strengthening to know that prayers are being said for the person who carries this constant concern. There were times when such assurance was of great comfort.

While the individual cases were not general knowledge, the public occasions certainly were, and the number of "official openings" mounted steadily through the years. These events may have been looked upon with a certain mockery as "political occasions" and official parties. But the feeling which prompted Bob to make each of these a special event lay in his desire to honour the Muskoka people who had worked for it and to give opportunity for the worthy celebration in the community of the new facility or service being enjoyed. Though ceremony might prevail and visiting dignitaries be accorded all due honour, there was always, at Bob's insistence, a family party as well as the appropriate ceremonies.

It became almost mandatory that each of these be honoured by a visit from a cabinet minister, so that nearly all the men who held cabinet positions during those years had paid an official visit to Muskoka. Naturally these visits were not confined to the official ceremony, the speeches and ribbon-cutting. Many included stops at Muskoka resorts, boat-rides on the lakes, or other of the special joys of Muskoka to make their stay more pleasant, and at the same time impress upon them the delights, and the needs, of this area.

It is not my intention to list the events so marked, or the additions to Muskoka during Bob's term of representation, except in most general terms.

There were many school openings, new buildings and additions to the old, as Muskoka's education system expanded. There were new buildings for the Lands and Forests, the Provincial Police, and municipal offices in several townships. There were new stretches of

Bob Boyer worked assiduously with Ontario Fire Marshal William Scott, Q.C., to convert the old Sanitarium facilities near Gravenhurst into the province's educational centre for firefighters. Several powerful cabinet ministers understandably wanted the new Ontario Fire College in their ridings, so the Member for Muskoka was justifiably proud of this accomplishment. Bob is third from the right. In the light coat beside him is friend and Gravenhurst lawyer Peter B. Stuart, Q.C. George Beard is first on the left. The others are Ontario's Fire Marshal, Deputy Fire Marshal, and Director of the College.

highway, and new bridges with them. These were not exclusively Bob's efforts, of course, but all required certain areas of co-operation with the department concerned, and their opening provided occasions with which he was pleased to be associated.

There was the institution of the Ontario Fire College, using the old Sanitarium buildings in Gravenhurst, an innovation and establishment in Muskoka with which Bob was deeply involved and which pleased him tremendously.

The opening of Arrowhead Park, north of Huntsville, was the culmination of a long quest to provide public recreational ground in Muskoka. The rapid development of the district had proceeded without providing for such facilities and yet the need for such was great and obvious. The acquisition was not accomplished without hours of planning and study.

The placing of Historic Site Markers in many Muskoka locations, and the ceremonies accompanying their unveiling gave Bob great delight, as it involved the study and research into early Muskoka history, a deep interest which he shared with his father. On these occasions Bob gave special care that his speech should honour the early settlers, and their present day descendants. In fact it was almost always his custom on a ceremonial occasion to make reference to the people whose early efforts and hopes had established the community.

It was a great pleasure that the first of Ontario's Historic Site Markers was placed in Muskoka, at Port Carling, and was unveiled by the Premier, the Honourable Leslie M. Frost, who is also a keen amateur historian.

But Bob has said that of all the things that were developed in Muskoka with his assistance, the one that brought him the greatest happiness and gratification was the opening of a road into the Wah-Wah-Taisee Reserve on Georgian Bay, near MacTier, bringing these Indian people into contact with their neighbours at the same time maintaining their homes and traditional heritage. Co-incidental with the road opening was the enlargement of the MacTier school, which provided extra accommodation for the boys and girls of the Reserve. Now, like every other Muskoka student, they would travel by bus to a large and well-equipped school, and return home in the afternoon.

It was not exactly a spoken agreement, but it became a part of the understanding in our home that Bob's obligations to his position as member took precedence over everything else. As much as possible this included my own participation in the events of Muskoka. There were times when it was not easy to choose between the requirements of a family of growing school children and the official duties. But a request or an invitation was never declined unless it was a physical impossibility to comply. Even then, it was remarkable how one could travel about the district to several events on one busy Saturday; or how, especially in Centennial summer, we could divide between us the exciting array of events to attend and enjoy.

High on the list of important things to do was the sharing with the people of Muskoka in their personal occasions of importance. The celebration of Golden Weddings, or special birthday parties, gave a unique opportunity for enlarging friendship and understanding. In the same way, Bob wished to share with friends on the sad family occasions. In this, whether in joy or sorrow, whether in family gatherings or local festivals, there was a desire to be with the people

Ontario's Premier John P. Robarts witnesses the swearing in of his nominee Robert Boyer as a vice-chairman of Ontario Hydro, in the cabinet office at Queen's Park.

he represented, to come to know them at times of jubilation or concern, to forge a closer bond of support among individuals and to strengthen the family spirit of Muskoka which has been our foundation since pioneer times.

THE HYDRO YEARS

In November 1962 Bob was asked by Premier John Robarts to join the Ontario Hydro Commission as second vice-chairman. This position is the government link with the Commission, held by an elected member and appointed by the Cabinet. It is also a very real responsibility in the administration of this large utility organization. Bob was a member of the Commission until the end of June 1971. At that time he had already announced his intention not to stand for re-election, and resigned also from Hydro. He had become first vice-chairman in 1969.

These were extremely demanding years, as it virtually added a third job to the two he was already carrying, that of elected member for Muskoka as well as editor of *The Herald-Gazette*. Even when the legislature was in recess the work at Hydro continued, necessitating being every week in Toronto.

While enlarging the workload, the new position also opened up a wider field of responsibility and experience. The extent and the advancement of the Hydro policy and operation in Ontario are tremendous. The decisions, such as those concerned with nuclear development, were vital and the consultations with other governmental bodies, municipal, Federal in Canada, and State in the U.S.A. presented a challenging task.

This also provided a rewarding experience of enlarging association, far beyond the headquarters on University Avenue; and included duties as well as ceremonial occasions in

Robert J. Boyer, MPP, First Vice-Chairman of Ontario Hydro, in his Toronto office on University Avenue. This serious work became a major focus for him, ranging from decisions on Hydro's plans to develop nuclear energy, to collaborating with public power utilities in the USA, the UK, and elsewhere in Canada.

Addressing the Hydro Awards Banquet, Robert Boyer as a public official emphasized his role in bringing attention and recognition to those who contributed to the life of the community – an extension of his work as a weekly newspaper editor in celebrating people's accomplishments in print.

every part of Ontario, in several bordering States, and in England. The wide circle of acquaintanceship, and the growing knowledge of the business of national growth was an enriching experience. It was paid for, of course, in long and often worrisome hours of consultation, reading and writing, and seemingly endless travel. But it was a good time, and the Hydro years have made a happy and gratifying memory.

Perhaps one of the happiest things about this time was the opportunity to share in honour to Muskoka citizens and enterprises. The Hydro Retirement and Safety Award dinners in this area were most special occasions. And the arrangement for plaques to recognize early hydro development in Bracebridge and in Wasdell Falls was a duty eagerly accepted.

But basically, this was a time of wider service when the interests of all Ontario and of her relationship with her neighbouring states became the arena of Bob's endeavours.

CHANGES

Inevitably the years between 1955 and 1971 saw radical changes in the life and work of a member of the Legislature, as in every other phase of activity.

During Bob's first few years, while the Honourable Leslie Frost was the Premier, the Legislature met for a few weeks each year, starting late in January, and proroguing just before Easter. At that time the whole House reflected the old Ontario pattern, the dignity of Mr. Frost, the respect for the authority of the Speaker. Debate was lively but, on the whole, civil. The House was a good place to be, whether as a participant or as a gallery guest.

It was probably a good time to be initiated into membership. At that time the average age of members was higher than it is today, and most members' wives spent part, or all, of the winter session in Toronto, (it follows that they too were older with less demanding home ties) so that the social life was more active. There was opportunity for groups to gather, husbands and wives, to find friendship and relaxation, and to enjoy the entertainment of the winter season. Mr. and Mrs. Frost were gracious leaders in such pleasant social activity.

During the years that the Honourable John Robarts was Premier the operation of the Legislature seemed to tighten to a more business-like and a more intensive pace. Sessions lasted longer (both as to the year and the daily hours). New legislation, embracing the social impact that was taking over the country, demanded more work in the preparation, in the consideration, and eventually in the administration. In the House there appeared the prevalent attitude that delights in vituperation and disregards authority.

The Davis regime, which began as Bob was preparing to leave the legislature, saw another change. The Premier brought about the technical developments of the '70s, the stress on expertise, the toughness of today's business world to the administration of the great and growing business of Canada's leading province. This is government by new, young men, who bring their own definite vitality and speed to the conduct and the concept of provincial management.

Changes too were occurring in the most specific area of Bob's responsibility, the management of Muskoka affairs. It was during his closing years as representative that he worked with others both in Muskoka and at Queen's Park for the change which was to bring District Government to Muskoka. It is fitting that this should have been the climax of his endeavours, because here he was able to see finally the establishment of Muskoka as a municipal entity.

The administration of 28 separate municipalities, with varying degrees of organization, each having to go separately through the member to Queen's Park for the settlement of its business contacts with the Province, early appeared to him as not good enough for a district expanding in economy and interest as well as population. The need for unity was also felt by many of the municipal leaders, and in bringing their concerns together and taking them to the provincial authorities, Muskoka people were able to sow the seeds that in time flowered into a truly District Government.

This was a most difficult time, because there was stubborn opposition to a plan which so many saw as taking the authority away from them. The truth, that government was to be seated right here in Muskoka, did not find as ready acceptance as the widespread rumour against the proposition Feelings ran very high, often alienating former friends. Bob was usually in the centre of the controversy, often the object of wild criticism. Had he not been truly devoted to the great dream of a better day for Muskoka government, and had he not been assured of the genuine support of the most experienced of the municipal leaders in Muskoka and of the Department of Municipal Affairs, he surely would have abandoned the long and discouraging struggle that led to Muskoka District Government in 1970.

As the beginning of his political career had seen Muskoka established as its own provincial riding, so the climax of it came with the elevation of his beloved District to the responsibility of its own government.

The occasion in October 1970 when His Honour the Lieutenant-Governor of Ontario attended to install the first Muskoka council, was a proud night for many of us, but for no one more than Bob Boyer, M.P.P. who had lived with the concept and striven patiently toward it for many months.

RETIREMENT

The announcement in the spring of '71 that he would not stand for re-election in the campaign expected later that year came as a surprise to most of Bob's Muskoka friends. With the conviction that one carries on a job to which he is committed, Bob had given no earlier intimation that this decision was in his mind, that he felt definitely that 16 years was a good term of office, and that the time had come for a new representative to carry on.

This would include the passing over of the heavy responsibility, the demands on time; as wells as the inestimable gratification and joy being the elected representative of the Muskoka people. The two sides of the coin are inseparable, and as both were fully experienced for the term of membership, both would also be relinquished as another would take over.

Like all decisions that Bob had been making through the years, striving for the good of his fellow citizens, this one was also a hard-won and carefully made decision. The personal element, of course, played some small part, for the routine schedule of his public life had accelerated with very little relaxation. However, we knew then and it has proved so during the succeeding year, that the restful suggestion of the word 'retirement' is misleading, for inevitably the local schedule of business and other commitments has equaled the former one of public service.

It was not for a rest that Bob gave up the work as a Member of the Legislature! Nor was it for any reason of discouragement or disappointment in this official work.

There had arisen in the government the slogan for a New Wave. Led by Mr. Robarts, who resigned at the height of a magnificent career as Premier, others of his caucus also handed over the reigns of a strong government to men and women of this new wave, ready and eager to carry the responsibility. It was in a move to serve Ontario and not themselves that these legislators made way for newcomers, and are now proudly watching the vigorous progress of their successors.

From the time that Muskoka Conservatives chose Frank Miller to be their candidate in May, 1971, Bob was preparing for the change in representation which was accomplished in October. During this time a warm and helpful relationship developed, as Bob and I enjoyed the privilege of launching Frank and Ann Miller on the way to provincial membership. Together at many Muskoka events, Bob introduced his successor with pride and confidence.

It reminded me of that stage in a relay race, when the second runner starts at a moderate pace and runs alongside the first runner during the transfer of the baton; and then, without any loss of momentum, the new goes full speed ahead! Sometimes it is not easy to see where that actual transfer takes place. With the election, the public new very well the date, October 21st. But perhaps only the runners knew how much had already been handed over to the new man.

It is fitting that here too I mention the cordial and mutually helpful relationship that grew and strengthened between Bob and Gordon Aiken during his federal membership. For the most part their terms coincided, and as they shared the same political philosophy and the same integrity of office and genuine concern for their constituents, their work was happily coordinated.

Retirement, as I have mentioned, has not meant leisure. Nor has it meant lessening of concern for Muskoka. In any endeavour in which Bob participates, primarily in newspaper work, his desire for the best for this District is devotedly maintained. And where, some years ago, it might have been Bracebridge that had his greatest concern, all Muskoka is now his home, and it is Muskoka as a part of the larger picture -- Ontario and Canada -- that he is now serving in his 'retired' capacity.

Bob 'out of uniform' and laughing with friends. When shown this picture recently, Robert Boyer, amazed at his informal attire, said "That had to be taken after I was no longer in public office!"

12

Sale of the Family Newspapers

R obert Boyer continued as publisher and editor of *The Herald-Gazette, The Muskoka Sun,* and other publications, including a large number of local history books, until the business of The Muskoka Publishing Company was sold in November 1976. It was like parting with the family jewels.

While Bob's mother Victoria (the 'Matriarch' of Patsy's pending novel) remained alive, her son would not have broached the subject of selling. The Boyers had earned worthy scars keeping the paper alive and in the forefront of community affairs. Vic would not have allowed the paper to be sold out of the family, but at age 90 she died. Patricia, for her part, felt time had come for Bob to retire with her from the weekly cycle of "Getting the paper out!" Not everyone was seized of the devil drive that kept Boyers working. Although she had become a Boyer by marriage, Patsy could still march to a different drummer. There were still books waiting to be read, several more to be written (including *The Matriarch*), plays to be seen, and many cathedrals in England and historic sites in North America yet to visit. With more to life, the newspaper and printing business would be sold. The question was, to whom?

Would the infant boy toasted in 1945 by the Weekly Newspaper Association as "a fourth generation of Boyer editors at Bracebridge" fulfill the prediction? Like his father, he had grown up in the business, operating a Linotype machine by age 14, acquiring skill in setting type by hand, preparing stereotype castings, making up pages. By his late teens, Bob and Patsy's son was also operating printing presses such as the Heidelberg and the large flat-bed Babcock hand-fed press on which he printed the weekly paper itself. Also he operated equipment for folding the papers, the paper cutting equipment, and a range of binding and book stitching equipment. Apart from become a printer he had moved in the direction of journalism, writing from early age a regular weekly column, news stories and feature articles.

Their son had also gained experience working on other papers, including in Ottawa and North Battleford, Saskatchewan. When he left Bracebridge for University, it was to study Journalism at Carleton University as the best way to get an education relevant to his newspaper future. It was clear he was following his father's footsteps, to become a local newspaper editor and in time, if the voters agreed, an elected representative. Their son accordingly made a written offer to purchase the business.

No one was clearer than Patricia in refusing even to consider her son's offer to continue the family publishing operation. She seemed not to have been the author of her earlier column about a mother needing the courage to see that her boy, in taking risks, is becoming a man. For the Boyer's son to take over the papers would, Patsy envisaged, lead to a situation where she and Bob would still be involved. It was time to move on! She displayed a clear sense of urgency about her need to have personal and private time, both with her husband whose energies and interests had been so demanded by others for so long, and for herself to read and write and garden.

Another would-be purchaser was Dr. Edward J. Britton, a university-trained man with a scholarly interest in mediaeval history and a personal attraction to the newspaper game. When he'd arrived in Bracebridge, Robert Boyer gave Ted Britton a job at *The Herald-Gazette,* and over time imparted to him things he knew about writing, editing and publishing a weekly newspaper. With two other employees of the newspaper, Dr. Britton had placed a second offer before Bob and Patsy for consideration.

The paper business was sold in November 1976, but neither to Ted Britton nor to their own son. The "What if...?" speculations about how the ensuing three decades might have unfolded differently for central Muskoka newspapers -- given the many ups and downs, arrivals and departures, new publishing ventures and costly failures, political careers and altered public reputations since that time – show the significance of the decision of 1976.

The agreement of sale was made with purchaser Hugh K.N. Mackenzie of Huntsville. The deal included both *The Herald-Gazette* and *The Muskoka Sun,* but also that Robert Boyer, as he himself said, "was expected to continue with the paper." In the end, both Robert and Patricia continued to write columns and features and be engaged with the paper under its new ownership. Dr. Britton started up a new paper some months later, and has since built a solid position as a no-holds-barred publisher and editorialist, with many publications in his operation. Mr. MacKenzie operated the papers for a period, then sold them. The new owner, Donald Smith, operated them and expanded both the facilities and the range of publications, until going bankrupt. From one week to the next, the flagship newspaper of central Muskoka, *The Herald-Gazette,* built upon the publishing traditions of both the Thomas Family and the Boyer Family, disappeared. There ws no last editorial, not even a "–30–", a printer's sign for "the end". Some employees of the paper started up a new publication, *The Muskoka Times,* which operated for a number of months before folding. A new sister publication, *Muskoka Vintage,* rose and fell. Donald Smith resumed publishing, starting a new Muskoka features periodical. Throughout the piece, many individual employees and numerous investors have lost considerable amounts of money. These paper wars had much of their cause, when one looks back, in the instability created by the decision to sell the Boyer Family newspapers in 1976. Hard feelings are created for cause, and feelings do not go away. They just go underground and wait for a chance to be expressed.

The ostensible reasons for the sale, moreover, were swallowed whole by the time things were done. The main idea behind terminating a four-generation publishing tradition was that, since the principal work of the publishing business still rested with Bob and Patsy, the cleanest way to 'retire' would be to sell off the operation and step back from it. Whether that was very realistic thinking, in a small town, is problematic. The result was certainly different, for despite the sale, Bob and Patsy remained involved. This included engagement by 'PMB', who found the concept of 'retirement' as illusory as when she'd written, in *My Bob . . . and Muskoka's* that it did not mean 'liesure' for people with abiding interest in Muskoka. Robert continued pretty much as anyone might have predicted for a man who loved, lived, and breathed newspapers and their creation. Patricia still wrote a weekly column, just as she had been doing for decades.

One such column by PMB, two years after the sale of the papers, appeared on October 4, 1978. Entitled 'Our Electronic Friends' it reflected her thoughts on the companionship people had with radio personalities in the golden age of radio, triggered by news of the death of Edgar Bergen, and just days before that, of Charles Godden. The former, "a keeper of kids' interests" as she called him, had brought to life the wooden puppet Charley McCarthy. The latter had been the 'Andy' half of the entertaining duo in the "Amos 'n Andy" radio show.

The final sentence of Patricia's October 1978 column read: " One of the costs of having so deeply enjoyed the golden age of radio is the personal involvement that means personal loss, now that time has brought us to the place that those in their prime then, are at the end of their lives." Could she have known that those final phrases were to be her very last words ever to appear in print?

Within two short years of the newspaper business having been sold out of the Boyer family, in order that Patricia's dream of personal freedom could be achieved, she died.

Local doctors had, with the off-hand way illnesses of mature women are too routinely dismissed, told her, in one case, that she "was a closet alcoholic" while another gave a diagnosis to the same symptoms as "early stages of dementia". Patricia Boyer was neither a drinker nor demented. She had been suffering in silence from a brain tumor.

In the years that followed, Robert never remarried. He was still in love with the vivacious librarian who had first captured his heart. Shorn of his newspapers, he now engaged in editorial work for others who owned the papers built up over generations by his family and himself. Drawing on his experience as editor of *The Herald-Gazette* and as editor of *The Muskoka Sun,* he also became associate editor of *The Algoma Anglican.* When the new publications *The Muskoka Times and Muskoka Vintage* came on the scene, he wrote articles for them about local history.

You could take the paper away from the man, but you could not take the man away from the paper.

Robert Boyer had been raised in a coat and jacket, and as an adult retained this uniform which he found comfortable and considered respectful of the public positions he held. Even on a private family trip to Northern Ontario, visiting Kakabeka Falls, he was most at ease in such dress. It is the barely visible smoking pipe he holds in his right hand that reveals him to be relaxed and having a happy time.

13

Five Sides of a Man

R obert Boyer, a man of parts, could be said to lead a compartmentalized life. Yet there is, in all that he does, an integrated dimension that rather shows these diverse elements not to really be separate, despite their differences, but rather parts of a whole. The man in full can be seen through five additional sides of activity – church life, service club activity, philanthropy, historical preservation, and support for public institutions.

Church as Part of RJB's Life

Robert was raised in a religious family, and he himself became active both in church life and the purposes of several closed societies.

In the Bracebridge United Church he was a leader in the committee which in 1951 had charge of remodeling the church sanctuary. Like his father George before him, Robert was Clerk of Session, the seniormost lay position in the local congregation of the Bracebridge United Church. Twice as a Commissioner to the General Council of United Church of Canada he attended these important national gatherings of Canada's largest Protestant denomination.

In January 1972 Robert was named organist and choir director of St. Thomas' Anglican Church in Bracebridge, continuing for more than a dozen years when his knowledge of church music, already extensive, had opportunity to expand further. He would happily slip into the church, for long hours of rehearsal, and for the sheer bliss of turning the notes on a sheet of music into the tremulous and powerful surges of overpowering harmony and uplifting majesty which only the organ can produce.

Robert Boyer's private pleasures included chocolates, cathedrals and puzzles. No more gleeful expression on his face has even been photographed than this shot where, against house rules he himself set about nobody going into the bottom layer of Black Magic chocolates until all those on the top layer were gone, his fingers reach for a fresh prize from the lower region of the renowned Black Box.

Bob and Patsy thoroughly enjoyed visits to cathedrals in England, an allied interest to their shared love of music, and their mutual explorations of life's spiritual dimension.

Puzzles, whether as word games or jig-saws, kept Bob's always engaged mind focused – affording a quiet interlude to reading, provided there was enough table space, as needed for this 1993 Christmas puzzle.

'Service Above Self' in Rotary

It would only have been surprising if Robert Boyer, raised up for public service and exulting in self-effacement, had not become a stalwart member of a local service club whose moto is to serve others ahead of self. He became a Rotarian in 1946, was president of the Bracebridge Rotary Club in 1973-74, and made a Paul Harris Fellow in recognition of his part in the expansion of the membership of the club.

Given his propensity to record history and write the stories of his community, it was also predictable that in 1986, when the Rotary Club of Bracebridge marked its 50th anniversary, he would write an engaging history about club accomplishments – from the street signs throughout the municipality to a community swimming pool, from exchange programs for students to the summer Rotary Fair – which he titled, *Fifty Years Above Self in Our Town.*

Robert was glad to see the entry of women into community service though Rotary, and felt pride in his niece Lynne Boyer Parks, the first-born child of his brother Wils and Dorothy Boyer, for becoming the first woman in Rotary. She joined the Etobicoke Rotary Club, which approved her application (although several members of the Club resigned in protest), but then headquarters of Rotary International in the United States overruled the local Club saying women could not qualify as members. It was front-page for *The Toronto Sun.* Bob's son Patrick, spoke in the House of Commons about the issue of his cousin seeking equality rights in Canada. Today many Rotary Clubs have women as their presidents.

In May of 1996, the Bracebridge Club honoured his half-century of Rotary service, and named Robert Boyer a life member.

Robert with Vicki, Alison and Patrick – Christmas '98 at The Pines. Since 1998, The Pines has been his residence. As a young Member of the Provincial Parliament Robert Boyer worked to establish The Pines as a residence for Muskoka seniors, when he discovered this District was the last in Ontario without such a facility.

Quietly Helping Muskokans Over 37 Years

Prominent philanthropists who donate their substantial wealth to benefit others are esteemed in society, but they seldom accomplish their good deeds alone. This is where quiet-spoken and knowledgeable individuals in the community enter the philanthropy picture.

In 1957 R. J. Boyer was asked by wealthy Montreal businessman and financier J. W. McConnell to be a director, together with the District Judge D.C. Thomas, Mrs. Thomas and two others, of a charitable foundation for Muskoka funded by Mr. McConnell in memory of his parents who had been Muskoka pioneers.

The McConnell Foundation is devoted to helping people of Muskoka who are in dire need and to assisting public institutions engaged in work of a charitable nature. R.J. Boyer continued in this work for the next 37 years, his knowledge of Muskoka District being of benefit to his fellow directors in their shared work to provide direct help within the community.

Finding Ways to Educate about History

The point of having history is to learn from it. That idea sounds great in general, but how does it become real in practice?

Bob and Patricia Boyer were founding directors of Bracebridge Historical Society in the early 1970s. Their enthusiasm and work in the initial stages led to creation of the excellent community museum, Woodchester Villa, which townspeople and many summer visitors now enjoy.

In 1982 Robert Boyer wrote and published a *Pictorial History of Woodchester Villa.* This superb story about the Bird Family and its octagonal house is one of the most handsome of all his booklets, seemingly inspired by the style and format of similar publications in the United Kingdom at the castles, cathedrals and homes of famous authors which Bob and Patsy so happily toured on visits there.

There are other ways, too, for making history known to people. While he had been MPP, Bob was responsible for the placing of about a score of Province of Ontario Historic Site Markers in locations throughout Muskoka District, including the very first in the province at Port Carling.

The idea for such markers was brought home by Leslie M. Frost from his vacation travels with his wife Gertrude through the history laden Civil War battlegrounds of the United States, where the Americans had been attentive and patriotic in commemorating historic deeds on the very ground where they had taken place. The premier of Ontario, a keen amateur historian who avidly collected local histories of any caliber about any Ontario city or hamlet, region or township, created the Ontario Historic Sites and

A great accomplishment for Muskoka's tourism industry, and a source of renewed pleasure for future generations discovering the joys of lake steamers, 'The Segwun' would sail again. At an official ribbon cutting ceremony are provincial MPP Robert Boyer, federal MP Gordon Aiken in top hat, Ontario's Minister of Tourism Hon. Brian L. Cathcart, and Peter B. Stuart of Gravenhurst.

Monuments Board. Bob Boyer assiduously supplied the Board with particulars of historic venues in the District he represented, and a year or so later proudly helped organize the official dedication ceremonies of the resulting plaques.

In the late 1970s a store on the main street of Bracebridge became vacant, and Robert saw an opportunity. The Herald-Gazette Bookstore soon opened, among its titles the many local histories which he had published through Muskoka Publishing Company Limited over the previous decade and more. In time the Bookstore was sold to Gil Scott, forming the basis for a greatly expanded bookstore, with art, at Scott's of Muskoka in the centre of town.

Raising Money for the Arena and the Public Library

In his community work following retirement from the Provincial Parliament, Robert Boyer continued to display the deep-seated instinct to serve others. One form in particular by which this side of him was expressed involved support for public institutions. For example, he sat for several years on the Board of the Royal Ontario Museum, a non-paid position of further public service to his province.

Closer to home, Bob headed financial campaigns for needed projects. One involved the renewal of the entrance, lobby and upper half of Bracebridge Memorial Community Centre arena. Another was to finance the spacious addition to Bracebridge Public Library, at which time the children's department was made a memorial to his wife Patricia.

The library expansion itself was a credit to the Town, the Library Board, and the architect. It respected the architectural integrity of the original Bracebridge Public Library building to which it was added, and reflected the red-brick construction tradition of authentic local look, a Bracebridge style jettisoned by all three levels of government, national corporations and many others in new construction and renovations alike from the late 1950s on. Fittingly the Bracebridge Public Library, temple of local learning, showed, like Robert Boyer, how one could honour the integrity of the past while moving forward.

Robert Boyer and Ontario's Premier Leslie M. Frost were ardent amateur historians, and when Frost began a program of historical commemorative plaques, creating the Archeological and Historic Sites Board of Ontario in the Department of Travel and Publicity, Bob worked to get many for Muskoka District, with the very first such plaque in all Ontario being unveiled at Port Carling.

In this scene, to the east of Muskoka at Lakefield, Ontario, a plaque commemorating Catharine Parr Traill was unveiled October 15th, 1958. Traill, a member of England's literary Strickland family, was a talented author who, with her husband Lieutenant Thomas Traill, struggled unsuccessfully for seven years in the 1830s to establish a profitable farm on bushland in Douro Township. Her best known book, The Backwoods of Canada, *was based on her pioneering experiences.*

The two women in this picture are Miss Anne Traill and Miss Anne Atwood, granddaughters of Catharine Parr Traill. Bearded and bespeckled is Robertson Davies, editor of The Peterborough Examiner *and himself a rising author at the time, beside Prof. T.F. McIlwraith of the Historic Sites Board.*

Robert Boyer, on the right, and Robertson Davies, both newspaper editors in central Ontario, enjoyed conversation about their literary adventures in publishing community newspapers.

Robert J. Boyer — Newspaper Publisher, Legislator, Local Historian, Church Organist, Author, Patriarch, Book Reader.

Older Boys of Bracebridge. When Bob Boyer was a young man he attended Ontario Older Boy' Parliament, whose sessions included training and experience in the conduct of a legislative assembly, and religious studies because in was a church-based organization to train young Canadians for high-minded public service. By the time he had been elected to the Ontario Legislative Assembly itself, Bob's son Patrick and Gary Hutton were two more Older Boys of Bracebridge attending the model parliament. Robert himself was back as 'Lieutenant Governor'. John Oldham was 'Premier'.

14

The Legacy of 'PMB'

Telling this story of RJB in terms of words and books, journalism and publishing, has woven in and out of the Bracebridge Public Library. He and his life partner PMB connected through love of literature, music, and one another as editor and librarian, man and woman. Theirs was a marriage of true minds. Their adventures are a shared story of single high-minded purpose. The legacy of PMB, like that of her husband, comes home, in the end, to books and the Bracebridge Public Library.

Patsy's book *Looking at Our Century* published in 1975, collected columns written by herself and others during the Town of Bracebridge's centennial year. In 1980, two years after her death, daughter Vicki gathered and published 89 of the best of these columns, "drawn from the period 1971-1978 but the distillation of situations experienced and concepts mellowed, of books read and perspectives expanded over three score and six years of a very full life". Timeless treasures, they appear in a book entitled *The March of Days*.

Patricia feeds one of the canine members of the Johnson family at Westlawn.

A work-in-progress at the time of Patricia's death, *The Matriarch*, had the ingredients to become an important Canadian novel, and her writing style the potential to make it so, especially in a land which, for all the other impediments women have faced, long has celebrated its female writers and stories about remarkable women. That it was never completed appears, in part, to have been due to the incessant demands on both her time and mental energies by the many community and church organizations in which she played such pivotal roles. That is also the legacy of Patricia Mary Boyer.

Active in church work, she became president of the Toronto Conference of United Church Women. An ardent believer in freedom of expression against tyranny, she was extremely active as founding president of the Bracebridge Chapter of Amnesty International. Concerned for the well-being and equality of those facing challenges and impediments, she was a founding member of the Victoria Street School in Bracebridge for children with mental disabilities.

There was more. A celebrant of the arts and their centrality in human societies, she was a founding member and first president of the highly successful Muskoka Arts & Crafts Show which for four decades since has been a summer highlight in central Muskoka. An alto, she was not only an active participant in the Bracebridge Choral Society but also a steady member of the United Church Choir in Bracebridge, a lamented loss to the Baptists where her mother Lillie was organist and choir director for decades.

There was even more. Adept as an instructor who relied upon students to work hard and figure things out as much as they could themselves, she began her teaching career at Bancroft in the 1930s (with return holiday visits driving her own car alone over muddy rutted roads to Bracebridge and back) later continuing as a supply teacher at Bracebridge High School.

Ruth Tinkiss, who as a girl had come to love books at librarian Patricia M. Johnson's Saturday morning 'Story Hour' in the Bracebridge Public Library, proposed creation of The Patricia M. Boyer Children's Library in 1986. Here she walks in a Bracebridge park with Robert Boyer.

A skilled interpreter of plays, whether in acting roles on stage or in the audience as theatre critic for the newspaper, she especially enjoyed orchestrating productions, and for a number of years was director of the annual Christmas pageant at Bracebridge United Church. One of the children she selected to play Virgin Mary became so enthralled with the role of an actress that she successful pursued a career on stage as an adult. "I got my start in theatre from Patricia Boyer," recalled richly talented Bracebridge actress Robin Knowles, who today continues her captivating roles at sold-out performances.

Patricia Boyer also deployed her devotion to children and spiritual life in the role of Superintendent of the Bracebridge United Church Sunday School for a number of years.

As a self-reliant woman, she was a member of the Bracebridge Business & Professional Women, sharing a bond with other women who stepped up and stepped out to make their own way in a world largely fashioned around the practices and preferences of males. Even so, she successfully merged her career with that of her husband Robert Boyer. It was a true merger, not a subversion, for they were equal partners in a mutual adventure that neither Bob nor Patsy could have experienced without the role and aptitudes of the willing other.

In her early career as librarian in Bracebridge, Patricia began 'The Story Hour'. At this Saturday morning event for youngsters of central Muskoka she selected stories from books, reading and explaining them with such dramatic flourish and excitement that captivated children followed their young minds and engaged emotions up onto the broad pathway of literature. In this way Patricia fulfilled the role of librarian as angel of knowledge, combining her joy in teaching with a relish for compelling narrative.

In 1986 the Bracebridge Library Board created The Patricia M. Boyer Children's Library, to serve newer generations and recognize their former librarian's invaluable contribution connecting children with literary adventures. Designation of the children's library in her honour was proposed by Ruth Tinkiss. As a young girl, Ruth had been one of those who keenly attended Patricia Johnson's Saturday morning 'Story Hour'. It was then and there that Ruth's life-long love affair with books was launched. "We waited all week for Saturday morning to come around again," she later recalled.

Creation of The Robert J. Boyer Reading Room in the same library means the human partnership between 'Patsy' and 'Bob', united both in human love and in their abiding devotion to literature, now achieves further symmetry in its institutional expression. In this way, their long associations with the Bracebridge Public Library, just like their own writing and indeed all literature itself, can endure to touch others, beyond the time the authors themselves, as she last wrote, "are at the end of their lives."

RJB and daughter Vicki, benefactor of The Robert J. Boyer Reading Room, seated at the Boyer Family home on Kimberley Avenue with marigolds and coloured leaves of autumn.

15

Recognition of Reading

With a lifetime of public service, Robert Boyer has been awarded a number of general recognitions for his contributions, including the Canada Confederation Centennial medal in 1967, the Queen's Silver Jubilee medal in 1977, and the Order of Ontario medal in 1987.

Other forms of recognition landed closer to specific or particular community services he rendered. One example of this came in 1980. Bob's decades-long journalistic endeavours found fitting recognition when the Canadian Community Newspapers Association presented him its 50-year Golden Pen Award.

A second example of such recognition, focused on what he had uniquely done, involved the Muskoka Lakes Association. While provincial member for Muskoka, Bob

A great-grandfather, in the presence of their mothers, instructs his five great-grandchildren on the skill of rolling cherries through a hole in the top of the table where they are enjoying a late summer picnic.

Boyer maintained close relations with summer residents, consulted their association executives, and attended annual meetings of the principal associations. In 1981, years after leaving public life, he received the first Robert W. Purves memorial award, given "for love and dedication to Muskoka" and presented at the annual meeting of the Muskoka Lakes Association.

The Muskoka Heritage Foundation came up with a great idea, when it created 'The Robert J. Boyer Award' to recognize, in turn, those who have significantly contributed to the "built heritage" of Muskoka District. A sister award, named for Wayland Drew is given for those preserving Muskoka's "natural heritage'. The Boyer trophy is a bronze casting of *The Muskoka Herald* building as in appeared in "the good old days' when a young Bob Boyer began his editor's career there, entering into his world of words at 27 Dominion Street past a cluster-globe street lamp and the then unstuccoed red-brick walls of this 1891 building.

The Robert J. Boyer Reading Room

Closer still, as a means of recognition, is the gesture which acknowledges not so much what he has done, but rather who he is. Because he is a man of words, in so many senses and dimension, how is one to recognize that?

On August 25th, 2003, the opening of The Robert J. Boyer Reading Room at the Bracebridge Public Library, substantially the gift of his daughter Victoria Billingsley of Inuvik, Edmonton and Bracebridge, accorded such a particular recognition. A Reading Room is a significant and most fitting honour, for it expresses both the love of a daughter and the gratitude of a community for a man and his world of words.

"Give heed to reading," wrote Paul to Timothy. The Robert J. Boyer Reading Room forms a new bond with a man who lived by words and the Word. The bond is with those who today and tomorrow will benefit from a room dedicated to the high art of reading.

Reading is even more than an art. It is an ethical act. To the Greeks 'ethics' was the word for character. Robert Boyer's character is inseparable from the majestic freedom of reading and his life-long marriage to the world of words.

As a man thinketh, so shall he live.

Robert Boyer goes for a stroll with his great-grandson Douglas Billingsley.